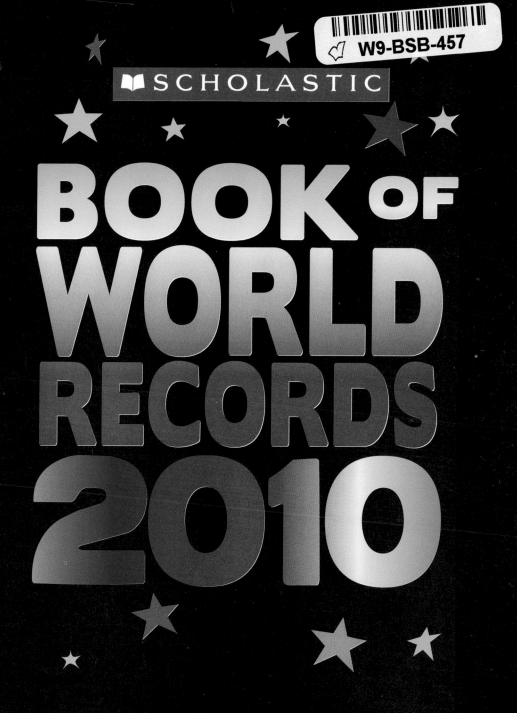

SCHOLASTIC

BOOK OF WORLD RECORDS 2010

BY JENIFER CORR MORSE
A GEORGIAN BAY BOOK

To Isabelle Nicole—May you always find wonder in the world.
—JCM

CREATED AND PRODUCED BY GEORGIAN BAY ASSOCIATES, LLC

GEORGIAN BAY STAFF
Bruce S. Glassman, Executive Editor
Jenifer Corr Morse, Photo Editor
Amy Stirnkorb, Designer

In most cases, the graphs in this book represent the top five record holders in each category. However, in some graphs, we have chosen to list well-known or common people, places, animals, or things that will help you better understand how extraordinary the record holder is. These may not be the top five in the category. Additionally, some graphs have fewer than five entries because so few people or objects reflect the necessary criteria.

ISBN-13: 978-0-545-16065-0
ISBN-10: 0-545-16065-0

10 9 8 7 6 5 4 3   09 10 11 12 13
Printed in the U.S.A.   40
First printing, September 2009

Due to the publication date, statistics are current as of August 2009.

CONTENTS

CONTENTS

POP CULTURE RECORDS

Television
Movies
Music
Magazines
Theater
Art

Highest-Paid TV Actor

CHARLIE SHEEN

Charlie Sheen gets $825,000 an episode for his role as Charlie Harper on the hit CBS sitcom *Two and a Half Men,* which he also helps produce. The Emmy-winning show is consistently one of the top-rated comedies each year. For this role, Sheen has been nominated for two Golden Globe Awards and two Emmy Awards. Before Sheen graced the TV screen, he appeared in many successful movies including *Platoon* (1986), *Major League* (1989), *Hot Shots!* (1991), and *Scary Movie 3* (2003). Sheen got his star on the Hollywood Walk of Fame in 1994.

6

Highest-Paid TV Actors

Money earned per episode during the 2008–2009 season, in US dollars

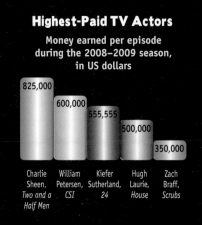

| 825,000 | 600,000 | 555,555 | 500,000 | 350,000 |
| Charlie Sheen, *Two and a Half Men* | William Petersen, *CSI* | Kiefer Sutherland, *24* | Hugh Laurie, *House* | Zach Braff, *Scrubs* |

Highest-Paid TV Actresses

THE DESPERATE HOUSEWIVES

Marcia Cross, Teri Hatcher, Felicity Huffman, and Eva Longoria Parker—the main cast of the hit show *Desperate Housewives*—each make $440,000 an episode. The ladies of Wisteria Lane are better known as Bree Hodge (Cross), Susan Mayer (Hatcher), Lynette Scavo (Huffman), and Gabrielle Solis (Longoria Parker) to television audiences. Executive producer Marc Cherry brought this nighttime soap to life in 2004, and since then the show has won seven Emmy Awards and three Golden Globes.

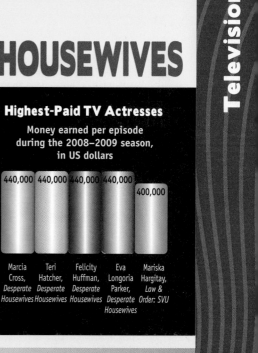

Highest-Paid TV Actresses

Money earned per episode during the 2008–2009 season, in US dollars

440,000	440,000	440,000	440,000	400,000
Marcia Cross, *Desperate Housewives*	Teri Hatcher, *Desperate Housewives*	Felicity Huffman, *Desperate Housewives*	Eva Longoria Parker, *Desperate Housewives*	Mariska Hargitay, *Law & Order: SVU*

Most Popular Television Show

AMERICAN IDOL TUESDAY

American Idol on Tuesday pulled in 16.1% of the viewing audience during the 2008 season. During the seventh season of the wildly popular singing competition, the show's contestants performed in front of judges Simon Cowell, Randy Jackson, and Paula Abdul. Once the field of contestants was narrowed down by the judges, viewers voted David Cook as the new American Idol with the majority of the 97.5 million votes cast. A spin-off of the UK's *Pop Idol*, *American Idol* premiered on Fox in 2002.

Most Popular Television Shows

Average audience percentage in 2008

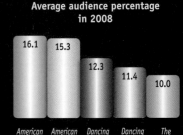

American Idol	American Idol Results	Dancing with the Stars	Dancing with the Stars Results	The Mentalist
16.1	15.3	12.3	11.4	10.0

8

Highest-Paid Talk Show Host

OPRAH WINFREY

Oprah Winfrey pulled in $275 million in 2008, making her the world's highest-paid entertainer. In total, she is worth more than $1.5 billion. Oprah's self-made millions have come mostly from her television show, which began in 1983. Since then, Oprah has been educating her viewers and helping her audience with tough social issues. The megastar is also involved in movies, television production, magazines, books, radio, and the Internet. In 2009, she will debut the Oprah Winfrey Network and begin a three-year deal with XM Satellite Radio.

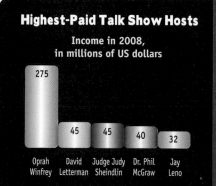

Highest-Paid Talk Show Hosts

Income in 2008, in millions of US dollars

Oprah Winfrey	David Letterman	Judge Judy Sheindlin	Dr. Phil McGraw	Jay Leno
275	45	45	40	32

TV Show with the Most Emmy Awards

FRASIER

Frasier—a hugely popular show that ran between 1993 and 2004—picked up 37 Emmy Awards during its 11 seasons. The sitcom focused on the life and family of psychiatrist Dr. Frasier Crane, played by Kelsey Grammer. His co-stars included David Hyde Pierce, John Mahoney, Peri Gilpin, and Jane Leeves. Some of the 37 awards the series won include Outstanding Comedy Series, Lead Actor in a Comedy Series, Supporting Actor in a Comedy Series, Directing in a Comedy Series, Editing, and Art Direction.

TV Shows with the Most Emmy Awards

Emmys won

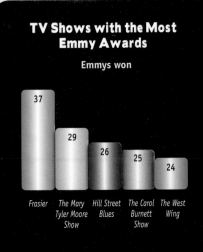

Frasier	The Mary Tyler Moore Show	Hill Street Blues	The Carol Burnett Show	The West Wing
37	29	26	25	24

TV Shows with the Most Consecutive Emmy Awards

THE DAILY SHOW WITH JON STEWART & THE AMAZING RACE

Two television shows—*The Daily Show with Jon Stewart* and *The Amazing Race*—are tied for the most consecutive Emmy wins with six each. Comedy Central's *The Daily Show* is a fake news program and has been hosted by Jon Stewart since 1999. The show picked up Emmys for Outstanding Variety, Music, or Comedy Series, and Outstanding Writing for Outstanding Variety, Music or Comedy Program. *The Amazing Race* on CBS has won the Emmy for Outstanding Reality-Competition Program since the award was first given in 2003. The show is hosted by Phil Keoghan and produced by Jerry Bruckheimer.

TV Shows with the Most Consecutive Emmy Awards

Emmys won

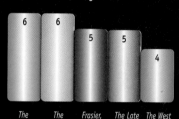

The Daily Show with Jon Stewart, 2003–2008	The Amazing Race, 2003–2008	Frasier, 1994–1998	The Late Show with David Letterman, 1998–2002	The West Wing, 2000–2003
6	6	5	5	4

Jerry Bruckheimer (left) and Phil Keoghan

Male Performer with the Most Emmy Awards

CARL REINER

Veteran actor Carl Reiner has won eight Emmy Awards since his acting career began in the 1950s. In 1957, Reiner picked up his first Emmy for his work on the comedy *Caesar's Hour*. A year later, he got his second award for *Sid Caesar Invites You*. Then, beginning in 1962, Reiner won three consecutive Emmys for his role on *The Dick Van Dyke Show*. Later, Reiner was recognized for his television writing with two awards in 1965 and 1967 for his work on *The Dick Van Dyke Show* and *The Sid Caesar Show*. Almost 30 years later, Reiner picked up an Emmy for a guest spot he did on the comedy *Mad About You*. Reiner continues to entertain audiences today, most recently with his role as Saul Bloom in the *Ocean's Eleven* movies.

Male Performers with the Most Emmy Awards

Emmys won

Carl Reiner	Ed Asner	Alan Alda	Art Carney	Billy Crystal
9	7	6	6	6

Female Performer with the Most Emmy Awards
CLORIS LEACHMAN

Since her acting career began almost 40 years ago, comedian Cloris Leachman has won eight Emmy Awards. Leachman won her first three awards between 1973 and 1975 for her role on *The Mary Tyler Moore Show*. In 1975, she also won an Emmy for her work on the variety show *Cher*. In 1984, she picked up another Emmy for her performance on the *Screen Actors Guild 50th Anniversary Celebration*. In 1998, Leachman grabbed an Emmy for her guest spot on *Promised Land*. And in 2002 and 2006, she won two statues for guest spots on *Malcolm in the Middle*. In 2008, Leachman danced her way back into the television spotlight with a stint on *Dancing with the Stars*.

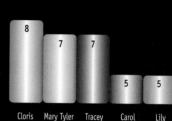

Female Performers with the Most Emmy Awards

Emmys won

Cloris Leachman	Mary Tyler Moore	Tracey Ullman	Carol Burnett	Lily Tomlin
8	7	7	5	5

13

Actor with the Most Oscar Nominations

JACK NICHOLSON

Jack Nicholson has been nominated for a record 12 Oscars during his distinguished career. He is one of only three men to have been nominated for an acting Academy Award at least once during five different decades. He was nominated for eight Best Actor awards for his roles in *Five Easy Pieces* (1970), *The Last Detail* (1973), *Chinatown* (1974), *One Flew Over the Cuckoo's Nest* (1975), *Prizzi's Honor* (1985), *Ironweed* (1987), *As Good As It Gets* (1997), and *About Schmidt* (2002). He was nominated for Best Supporting Actor for *Easy Rider* (1969), *Reds* (1981), *Terms of Endearment* (1983), and *A Few Good Men* (1992). Nicholson picked up statues for *One Flew Over the Cuckoo's Nest, Terms of Endearment*, and *As Good As It Gets*.

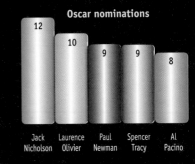

Actors with the Most Oscar Nominations

Oscar nominations

Jack Nicholson	Laurence Olivier	Paul Newman	Spencer Tracy	Al Pacino
12	10	9	9	8

Actress with the Most Oscar Nominations
MERYL STREEP

Meryl Streep is the most nominated actress in the history of the Academy Awards with 15 chances to win a statue. Her first nomination came in 1979 for *The Deer Hunter,* and was followed by *Kramer vs. Kramer* (1980), *The French Lieutenant's Woman* (1981), *Sophie's Choice* (1983), *Silkwood* (1983), *Out of Africa* (1985), *Ironweed* (1987), *A Cry in the Dark* (1988), *Postcards From the Edge* (1990), *The Bridges of Madison County* (1995), *One True Thing* (1998), *Music of the Heart* (1999), *Adaptation* (2002), *The Devil Wears Prada* (2006), and *Doubt* (2008). Streep won her first Academy Award for *Kramer vs. Kramer,* and followed with a second win for *Sophie's Choice.*

Actresses with the Most Oscar Nominations

Oscar nominations

Meryl Streep	Katharine Hepburn	Bette Davis	Geraldine Page	Greer Garson
15	12	10	8	7

15

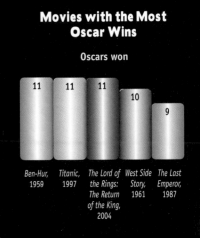

The cast of *The Lord of the Rings*
(Peter Jackson in front)

Movies with the Most Oscars

BEN-HUR, TITANIC, &
THE LORD OF THE RINGS:
THE RETURN OF THE KING

The only three films in Hollywood history to win 11 Academy Awards are *Titanic*, *Ben-Hur*, and *The Lord of the Rings: The Return of the King*. Some of *Titanic*'s Oscars include Best Cinematography, Visual Effects, and Costume Design. Some of the Oscar wins for *Ben-Hur*—a biblical epic based on an 1880 novel by General Lew Wallace—include Best Actor (Charlton Heston) and Director (William Wyler). *The Lord of the Rings: The Return of the King* is the final film in the epic trilogy based on the works of J.R.R. Tolkien. With 11 awards, it is the most successful movie in Academy Awards history because it won in every category in which it was nominated. Some of these wins include Best Picture, Director (Peter Jackson), and Costume Design.

Movies with the Most Oscar Wins

Oscars won

11	11	11	10	9
Ben-Hur, 1959	Titanic, 1997	The Lord of the Rings: The Return of the King, 2004	West Side Story, 1961	The Last Emperor, 1987

16

Actor with the Most MTV Movie Awards

JIM CARREY

Jim Carrey has won ten MTV Movie Awards since the television station began awarding them in 1992. He has won the award for Best Comedic Performance five times for his roles in *Dumb & Dumber* (1995), *Ace Ventura II: When Nature Calls* (1996), *The Cable Guy* (1997), *Liar Liar* (1998), and *How the Grinch Stole Christmas* (2001). Carrey won the award for Best Male Performance twice for *Ace Ventura II: When Nature Calls* and *The Truman Show* (1999). He also won awards for Best Kiss for *Dumb & Dumber*, Best Villain for *The Cable Guy*, and the MTV Generation Award in 2006.

Actors with the Most MTV Movie Awards

Awards won

Jim Carrey	Mike Myers	Peter Jackson	Adam Sandler	Brad Pitt
10	7	5	5	4

Uma Thurman

Actresses with the Most MTV Movie Awards
ALICIA SILVERSTONE & UMA THURMAN

Alicia Silverstone and Uma Thurman are tied for the most MTV Movie Awards with four statues apiece. Silverstone won her first two awards— Best Villain and Breakthrough Performance—in 1994 for her movie *The Crush*. She picked up two more in 1996—Best Female Performance and Most Desirable Female—for her role in *Clueless*. Thurman won a Best Dance Sequence award in 1995 for *Pulp Fiction*. She won Best Female Performance and Best On-Screen Duo (with Sandra Bullock) in 2004 for *Kill Bill I*. A year later she picked up the Best Fight award for *Kill Bill II*.

Actresses with the Most MTV Movie Awards

Awards won

Alicia Silverstone	Uma Thurman	Drew Barrymore	Kirsten Dunst	Cameron Diaz
4	4	3	3	3

18

Actress with the Highest Average Box-Office Gross
KEIRA KNIGHTLEY

Actress Keira Knightley is a safe bet for investors—her movies average more than $123.8 million each at the box office. Her 14 major movies have a combined box office gross of $1.72 billion in the United States. Her most successful movies have been *Pirates of the Caribbean: Dead Man's Chest* ($432.3M), *Star Wars Episode I: The Phantom Menace* ($431.1M), *Pirates of the Caribbean: At World's End* ($309.4M), and *Pirates of the Caribbean: The Curse of the Black Pearl* ($305.4M).

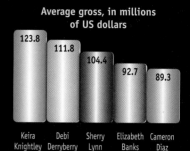

Actresses with the Highest Average Box-Office Gross

Average gross, in millions of US dollars

Keira Knightley	Debi Derryberry	Sherry Lynn	Elizabeth Banks	Cameron Diaz
123.8	111.8	104.4	92.7	89.3

Actor with the Highest Career Box-Office Earnings

FRANK WELKER

Frank Welker's movies have a combined total gross of $4.95 billion. Although movie fans might not recognize Welker's name or face, they would probably recognize one of his voices. Welker is a voice actor, and has worked on 89 movies in the last 25 years. Some of his most famous voices include Megatron, Curious George, and Scooby-Doo. Welker's most profitable movies include *How the Grinch Stole Christmas*, *Godzilla*, and *101 Dalmatians*.

20

Actors with the Highest Career Box-Office Earnings

Earnings, in billions of US dollars*

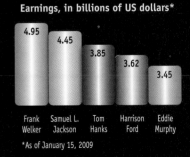

Frank Welker	Samuel L. Jackson	Tom Hanks	Harrison Ford	Eddie Murphy
4.95	4.45	3.85	3.62	3.45

*As of January 15, 2009

Top-Grossing Animated Movie
SHREK 2

Since it opened in May 2004, *Shrek 2* has brought in more than $919 million worldwide. The second movie in the *Shrek* series starred Mike Myers as Shrek, Cameron Diaz as Princess Fiona, Eddie Murphy as Donkey, and Antonio Banderas as Puss-in-Boots. It was the eighth highest-grossing opening weekend ever, earning $128.9 million in just three days. It is also the ninth-biggest opening day in history with $94.1 million. *Shrek 2* was nominated for an Oscar, a Golden Globe, two Grammy Awards, and four Kids' Choice Awards.

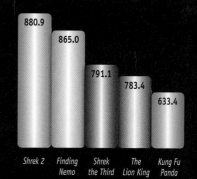

Top-Grossing Animated Movies

Total worldwide gross, in millions of US dollars

Shrek 2	Finding Nemo	Shrek the Third	The Lion King	Kung Fu Panda
880.9	865.0	791.1	783.4	633.4

Movie with the Most Successful Opening Weekend

THE DARK KNIGHT

On July 18, 2008, *The Dark Knight* opened in theaters and pulled in $158.4 million in just one weekend. The blockbuster movie, which is the sequel to *Batman Begins*, stars Christian Bale as Batman, Maggie Gyllenhaal as Rachel Dawes, Aaron Eckhart as Harvey Dent, and Heath Ledger as The Joker. *The Dark Knight* was released in 4,366 theaters and broke the record for a movie's largest release. The movie brought in $67.1 million on its opening day, with $18.5 million coming from midnight screenings. Heath Ledger won a Golden Globe and an Oscar posthumously for his role in the film.

Movies with the Most Successful Opening Weekends

Weekend earnings, in millions of US dollars

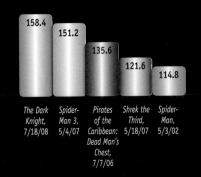

158.4	151.2	135.6	121.6	114.8
The Dark Knight, 7/18/08	Spider-Man 3, 5/4/07	Pirates of the Caribbean: Dead Man's Chest, 7/7/06	Shrek the Third, 5/18/07	Spider-Man, 5/3/02

Top-Grossing Movie

TITANIC

Directed by James Cameron in 1997, *Titanic* has grossed more than $600 million in the United States and more than $1.8 billion worldwide. This action-packed drama/romance is set aboard the White Star Line's lavish *RMS Titanic* in 1912. The two main characters, wealthy Rose DeWitt Bukater and poor immigrant Jack Dawson—played by Kate Winslet and Leonardo DiCaprio—meet, and fall in love, before the *Titanic* strikes an iceberg on the night of April 14, 1912, and sinks into the North Atlantic.

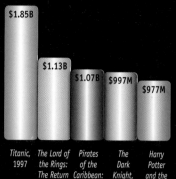

Top-Grossing Movies

Total worldwide gross, in US dollars

Movie	Gross
Titanic, 1997	$1.85B
The Lord of the Rings: The Return of the King, 2003	$1.13B
Pirates of the Caribbean: Dead Man's Chest, 2006	$1.07B
The Dark Knight, 2008	$997M
Harry Potter and the Sorcerer's Stone, 2001	$977M

23

Top Moviegoing Country

UNITED STATES

American moviegoers spend more than $9.2 billion each year on trips to the big screen. The average American sees about four movies annually. That equals about 1.21 billion admissions annually, with an average ticket price of $7.16. Some 600 movies are released throughout the country each year. When a new movie is released, it runs in theaters for about eight weeks and is shown on about 2,000 screens.

24

Top Moviegoing Countries

2008 box office revenue, in US dollars

USA	UK	Japan	France	Germany
9.22B	1.60B	1.42B	1.31B	904M

Country with the Most Movie Screens
UNITED STATES

There are about 38,834 movie screens located in nearly 6,000 movie theaters throughout the United States. About 636 screens are at drive-ins, and the other 38,159 screens are indoor theaters. Since the first permanent electric theater opened in 1902, Americans have flocked to the big screen. Megaplexes, or large movie theaters that show several movies at the same time, are the most popular type of theater in the country. Approximately 1.21 billion movie tickets are sold in the United States each year.

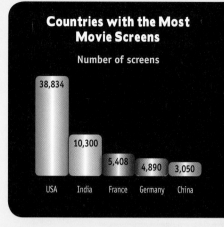

Countries with the Most Movie Screens

Number of screens

USA	India	France	Germany	China
38,834	10,300	5,408	4,890	3,050

Top-Earning Actor

WILL SMITH

While churning out hit after hit, Will Smith earned $80 million in 2008. Smith released *I Am Legend* at the end of 2007, and it was the most successful December release ever, taking in $77.2 million for the month. Its final worldwide gross was $585 million. In July 2008, Smith starred in *Hancock,* which went on to earn more than $624 million. Some of Smith's other highly successful movies include *Independence Day* (1996), *Men in Black* (1997), and *Hitch* (2005). Smith's combined box-office receipts total $5.68 billion.

Top-Earning Actors

2008 earnings, in millions of US dollars

Will Smith	Johnny Depp	Eddie Murphy	Mike Myers	Leonardo DiCaprio
80	72	55	55	45

Top-Earning Actress

CAMERON DIAZ

Thanks to a few successful movie roles, Cameron Diaz earned $50 million in 2008. In May of 2007, Diaz again lent her voice to Princess Fiona in *Shrek the Third*. This latest *Shrek* installment went on to earn $798.5 million worldwide. Then, Diaz released *What Happens in Vegas*—a romantic comedy with co-star Ashton Kutcher—in May 2008. This movie earned $219 million worldwide. Diaz commands one of the highest actress salaries in Hollywood, earning between $10 and $20 million per picture. Some of her other very successful movies include *The Mask* (1994), *There's Something About Mary* (1998), and *Charlie's Angels: Full Throttle* (2003).

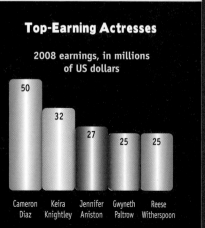

Top-Earning Actresses

2008 earnings, in millions of US dollars

Cameron Diaz	Keira Knightley	Jennifer Aniston	Gwyneth Paltrow	Reese Witherspoon
50	32	27	25	25

27

Highest Animated Film Budget

WALL-E

Disney went all out with its 2008 creation *WALL-E*, giving producers a $180 million budget to work with. The film went on to win an Oscar, a Golden Globe, a Grammy, and a Hollywood Film Award. The movie's main character is a cleaning robot whose name stands for "Waste Allocation Load Lifter Earth-class." WALL-E, voiced by Ben Burtt, and his robot girlfriend EVE, voiced by Elissa Knight, eventually help the human race return to Earth. The movie, which was produced by Pixar Studios, earned $63 million on its opening weekend.

28

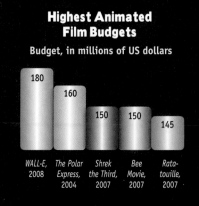

Highest Animated Film Budgets

Budget, in millions of US dollars

WALL-E, 2008	The Polar Express, 2004	Shrek the Third, 2007	Bee Movie, 2007	Rata- touille, 2007
180	160	150	150	145

Highest Movie Budget

PIRATES OF THE CARIBBEAN: AT WORLD'S END

With a budget of $300 million, the creators of *Pirates of the Caribbean: At World's End* spent the most money in movie history. And all of that money seems to have paid off. The third installment of the *Pirates* series opened in May 2007 and has since earned more than $960 million worldwide. It is the fifth-highest-grossing movie worldwide, and was the fourth-highest domestic gross in 2007. The Jerry Bruckheimer blockbuster starred Johnny Depp as Captain Jack Sparrow, Orlando Bloom as Will Turner, and Keira Knightley as Elizabeth Swann.

Highest Movie Budgets

Budget, in millions of US dollars

$300	$270	$258	$230	$225
Pirates of the Caribbean: At World's End, 2007	Superman Returns, 2006	Spider-Man 3, 2007	Quantum of Solace, 2008	Pirates of the Caribbean: Dead Man's Chest, 2006

29

Bestselling DVD of All Time

FINDING NEMO

Disney's favorite fish tale, *Finding Nemo*, has become the bestselling DVD of all time with more than $320.4 million in sales. The animated movie was released in 2003 and tells the story of a clownfish named Marlin, and his journey to find his young son, Nemo. Several funny celebrities lent their voices to the cast of characters, including Ellen Degeneres as Dory, Albert Brooks as Marlin, Brad Garrett as Bloat, and Allison Janney as Peach. *Finding Nemo* also won many awards, including an Oscar for Best Animated Feature in 2004.

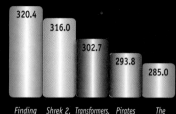

Bestselling DVDs of All Time

Revenue, in millions of US dollars

320.4	316.0	302.7	293.8	285.0
Finding Nemo, 2003	Shrek 2, 2004	Transformers, 2007	Pirates of the Caribbean: Dead Man's Chest, 2006	The Incredibles, 2005

Top-Selling DVD of 2008

THE DARK KNIGHT

The Dark Knight—the second installment of the new *Batman* saga—has sold almost 12 million copies since it was released on DVD on December 9, 2008. The film set a sales record when it sold more than 3 million copies on its first day of release. The thriller tells the story of Batman's battle with the villainous Joker. *The Dark Knight* stars Christian Bale as Batman, Heath Ledger as The Joker, Aaron Eckhart as Harvey Dent, and Maggie Gyllenhaal as Rachel Dawes. The film was also popular with critics, winning several Golden Globe, Screen Actors Guild, People's Choice, and American Film Institute awards.

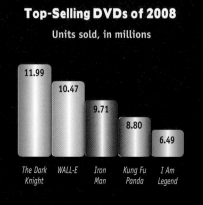

Top-Selling DVDs of 2008

Units sold, in millions

The Dark Knight	WALL-E	Iron Man	Kung Fu Panda	I Am Legend
11.99	10.47	9.71	8.80	6.49

Highest-Paid Director/Producer

JERRY BRUCKHEIMER

Movie and television producer Jerry Bruckheimer earned $145 million in 2008. Some of Bruckheimer's major movie successes for the year include *Pirates of the Caribbean: At World's End* and *National Treasure: Book of Secrets*. On the small screen, he produces some of the most popular television dramas, including *CSI: Crime Scene Investigation, Without a Trace, Cold Case*, and *CSI: Miami*. He has also won three Emmy Awards for *The Amazing Race*.

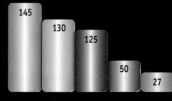

Highest-Paid Director/Producers

Income in 2008, in millions of US dollars

145	130	125	50	27
Jerry Bruckheimer	Steven Spielberg	Tyler Perry	George Lucas	Judd Apatow

Leona Lewis

Most Downloaded Song of 2008
"BLEEDING LOVE"

British pop star Leona Lewis is mighty popular—her song "Bleeding Love" was downloaded 3.42 million times in 2008. The singer, who got her big break on the reality competition *The X Factor*, saw her smash hit top more than thirty international music charts. And Lewis has set several other sales records in her short career. She had the fastest-selling debut album in the UK in 2007 when *Spirit* sold 375,000 copies in just one week. When *Spirit* entered the Billboard 200 chart at number one in the United States, Lewis became the first solo British artist to accomplish that with a debut album.

Most Downloaded Songs of 2008

Number of downloads, in millions

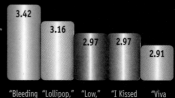

3.42	3.16	2.97	2.97	2.91
"Bleeding Love," Leona Lewis	"Lollipop," Lil Wayne	"Low," Flo Rida	"I Kissed a Girl," Katy Perry	"Viva La Vida," Coldplay

33

Most Downloaded Recording Artist of 2008

RIHANNA

With more than 9.9 million songs sold, Rihanna became the most downloaded artist of 2008. Since her debut song "Pon de Replay" hit the radio in 2005, Rihanna has scored five Billboard Hot 100 hits with "SOS," "Umbrella," "Disturbia," "Live Your Life," and "Take a Bow." She is only the second female solo artist to achieve this during this decade. In 2008, Rihanna became the first singer from Barbados to win a Grammy Award. She picked up the statue for Best Rap Collaboration for her hit "Umbrella." Her three albums—*Music of the Sun*, *A Girl Like Me*, and *Good Girl Gone Bad*—have sold more than 11 million copies worldwide.

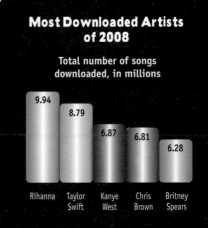

Most Downloaded Artists of 2008

Total number of songs downloaded, in millions

Rihanna	Taylor Swift	Kanye West	Chris Brown	Britney Spears
9.94	8.79	6.87	6.81	6.28

Bestselling Digital Album of All Time
VIVA LA VIDA

Coldplay's *Viva La Vida or Death and All His Friends* album has been downloaded more than 617,000 times since its release in 2008. Part of the album's major online success is due to the fact that its title track—"Viva La Vida"—was initially only available as a download on iTunes. The song reached number one on the Billboard Hot 100 and UK Singles charts. In the summer of 2008, Coldplay launched the *Viva La Vida* tour to promote the album, and the band received seven Grammy nominations, including Album of the Year.

Bestselling Digital Albums of All Time

Total number of downloads

Viva La Vida, Coldplay	Continuum, John Mayer	Back To Black, Amy Winehouse	Daughtry, Daughtry	Sleep Through The Static, Jack Johnson
617,000	386,000	352,000	346,000	325,000

Mariah Carey

Most Downloaded Music Video of 2008
"TOUCH MY BODY"

Mariah Carey's "Touch My Body" video was downloaded almost 7.4 million times in 2008. The hit song landed on the Billboard Hot 100, making it her eighteenth number-one single—a feat unsurpassed by any other solo artist in history. To celebrate this amazing accomplishment, the Empire State Building was lit with white, pink, and purple lights to resemble the album cover. The single came off Carey's eleventh studio album, $E=MC^2$, and was released in April of 2008. The album debuted at number one on the Billboard 200 and sold more than 463,000 copies during its first week.

36

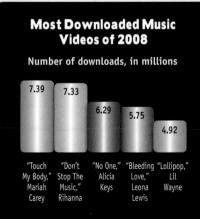

Most Downloaded Music Videos of 2008

Number of downloads, in millions

7.39	7.33	6.29	5.75	4.92
"Touch My Body," Mariah Carey	"Don't Stop The Music," Rihanna	"No One," Alicia Keys	"Bleeding Love," Leona Lewis	"Lollipop," Lil Wayne

United States' Bestselling Recording Group
THE BEATLES

The Beatles have sold 170 million copies of their albums in the United States since their first official recording session in September 1962. In the two years that followed, they had 26 Top 40 singles. John Lennon, Paul McCartney, George Harrison, and Ringo Starr made up the "Fab Four," as the Beatles were known. Together they recorded many albums that are now considered rock masterpieces, such as *Rubber Soul, Sgt. Pepper's Lonely Hearts Club Band*, and *The Beatles.* The group broke up in 1969. In 2001, however, their newly released greatest hits album—*The Beatles 1*—reached the top of the charts. One of their best-known songs—"Yesterday"—is the most recorded song in history, with about 2,500 different artists recording their own versions.

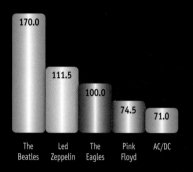

United States' Bestselling Recording Groups

Millions of albums sold

The Beatles	Led Zeppelin	The Eagles	Pink Floyd	AC/DC
170.0	111.5	100.0	74.5	71.0

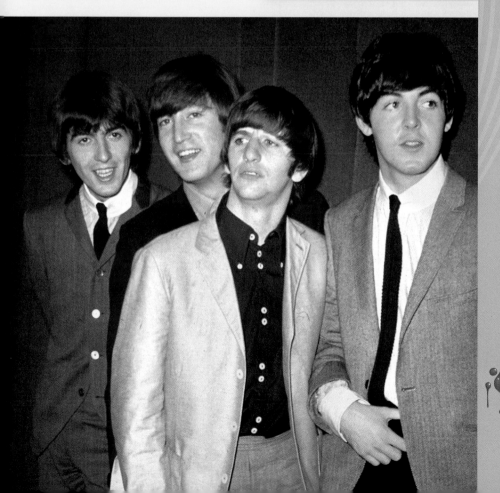

United States' Bestselling Male Recording Artist

GARTH BROOKS

Garth Brooks has sold 128 million albums since his professional career began in 1989. Brooks's career skyrocketed in 1991, when his third album—*Ropin' the Wind*—became the first country music album to debut on the top of the pop charts. From 1996 to 1999, Garth's tour stopped at 350 venues in 100 cities. More than 5.3 million tickets were sold, and it is considered one of the most successful tours in history. When the tour finished, Garth released his *Double Live* CD, and it became the bestselling live album ever. In all, Brooks has released 31 albums to date, and has won 15 Academy of Country Music Awards.

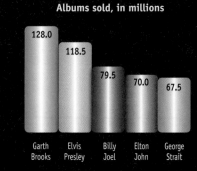

United States' Bestselling Male Recording Artists

Albums sold, in millions

Garth Brooks	Elvis Presley	Billy Joel	Elton John	George Strait
128.0	118.5	79.5	70.0	67.5

United States' Bestselling Female Recording Artist
BARBRA STREISAND

Barbra Streisand has sold almost 71 million copies of her work during her 39 years as a singer. She has recorded more than 50 albums and has more gold albums—or albums that have sold at least 500,000 copies—than any other entertainer in history. Streisand has 47 gold albums, 28 platinum albums, and 13 multiplatinum albums. Some of her recordings include "I Finally Found Someone" (1996), "Tell Him" (1997), and "If You Ever Leave Me" (1999). Some of her best-known film work includes roles in *Funny Girl*, *The Way We Were*, *Yentl*, and *Meet the Fockers*. Streisand has won 10 Grammys, 2 Academy Awards, 6 Emmy Awards, and 11 Golden Globes.

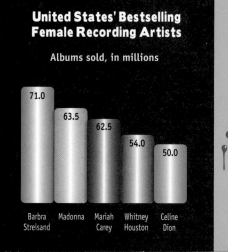

United States' Bestselling Female Recording Artists

Albums sold, in millions

Barbra Streisand	Madonna	Mariah Carey	Whitney Houston	Celine Dion
71.0	63.5	62.5	54.0	50.0

Top-Earning Male Singer

50 CENT

50 Cent earned $150 million in 2008, primarily from the sales of his latest albums—*Curtis* and *TOS: Terminate On Sight*. He also earned millions from the sale of his stake in Formula 50—a vitamin-water drink recently purchased by Coca-Cola. The rapper's big break came in 2003 with the release of "Get Rich or Die Tryin'," which debuted at number one on the Billboard 200 chart. He released *The Massacre* in 2005, and became the first solo artist with three songs in the Billboard Top 5 in the same week—"Candy Shop," "Disco Inferno," and "How We Do."

40

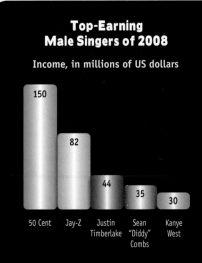

Top-Earning Male Singers of 2008

Income, in millions of US dollars

50 Cent	Jay-Z	Justin Timberlake	Sean "Diddy" Combs	Kanye West
150	82	44	35	30

Top-Earning Female Singer

BEYONCÉ

Beyoncé pulled in $80 million in 2008 with combined earnings from music sales, endorsement deals, and her clothing line. During her 2007 *The Beyoncé Experience* concert tour, she had more than $50 million in ticket sales. In late 2008, she released the album "I Am...Sasha Fierce," which has already produced two hit singles: "If I Were A Boy" and "Single Ladies (Put A Ring On It)." Beyoncé is also the spokeswoman for several brands—including L'Oreal and American Express—which bring in millions annually.

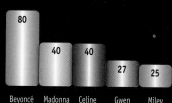

Top-Earning Female Singers of 2008

Income, in millions of US dollars

Beyoncé	Madonna	Celine Dion	Gwen Stefani	Miley Cyrus
80	40	40	27	25

Most Listened-To Radio Song of 2008

NO ONE

Alicia Keys' hit song "No One" reached more than 3.09 million listeners on the airways in 2008. The song was featured on Key's third studio album—*As I Am*—and reached number one on the Billboard Hot 100. It was her third single to achieve the number-one spot. At the 2008 Grammy Awards, Keys won Best Female R&B Performance and Best R&B Song for "No One." She also won two American Music Awards for her *As I Am* album, which sold about 4 million copies in the United States. During her career, Keys has sold more than 30 million albums worldwide.

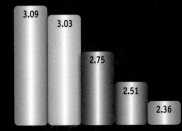

Most Listened-To Radio Songs of 2008

Number of listeners, in millions

"No One," Alicia Keys	"Low," Flo Rida	"Bleeding Love," Leona Lewis	"Apologize," Timbaland	"Lollipop," Lil Wayne
3.09	3.03	2.75	2.51	2.36

Bestselling Album of 2008
THA CARTER III

Tha Carter III—released by Lil Wayne on June 10, 2008—sold more than 2.87 million copies during 2008. It sold more than 1 million copies in its first week, and was certified as double platinum a month later. The album's first single, "Lollipop," reached number one on the Billboard Hot 100. Lil Wayne also led the Grammy nominations that year, with eight. He won four, including Best Rap Song and Best Rap Album. At the end of 2008, Lil Wayne became the first artist to be named MTV Man of the Year.

Bestselling Albums of 2008
Number of albums sold, in millions

Album	Millions sold
Tha Carter III, Lil Wayne	2.87
Viva La Vida, Coldplay	2.14
Fearless, Taylor Swift	2.11
Rock N Roll Jesus, Kid Rock	2.02
Black Ice, AC/DC	1.92

43

World's Top Earning Tours
BON JOVI

During 2008, Bon Jovi earned more than $210 million from its *Lost Highway* concert tour, which sold out all ten shows. Their *Lost Highway* album—the group's first stab at country music—debuted at number one on the Billboard charts and sold more than 290,000 copies during its first week. Band members include lead singer Jon Bon Jovi, guitarist Richie Sambora, keyboardist David Bryan, and drummer Tico Torres. Since the band formed in 1983, they have sold more than 120 million albums worldwide.

44

World's Top Earning Tours

Earnings, in millions of US dollars

Bon Jovi	Bruce Springsteen & the E Street Band	Madonna	The Police	Celine Dion
210	204	162	150	91

Act with the Most Country Music Awards

GEORGE STRAIT

George Strait has won a whopping 22 Country Music Awards and has been nicknamed the "King of Country" for all of his accomplishments in the business. He won his first CMA award in 1985, and his most recent in 2008. In addition to his many awards, Strait holds the record for the most number one hits on the Billboard Hot Country Songs with 44. He also has 38 hit albums, including 12 multi-platinum and 22 platinum records. He was inducted into the Country Music Hall of Fame in 2006.

Acts with the Most Country Music Awards

Total awards won

George Strait	Brooks & Dunn	Vince Gill	Alan Jackson	Garth Brooks
22	19	18	16	11

45

Musician with the Most MTV Video Music Awards

MADONNA

Madonna has won 20 MTV Video Music Awards since the ceremony was first held in 1984. She has won four Cinematography awards, three Female Video awards, three Directing awards, two Editing awards, and two Art Direction awards. She also picked up single awards for Video of the Year, Choreography, Special Effects, and Long Form Video, as well as a Viewer's Choice and a Video Vanguard Award. Madonna's award-winning videos include "Papa Don't Preach," "Like a Prayer," "Express Yourself," "Vogue," "Rain," "Take a Bow," "Ray of Light," and "Beautiful Stranger."

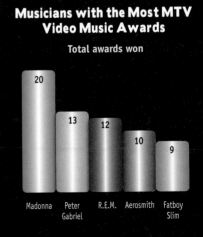

Musicians with the Most MTV Video Music Awards

Total awards won

Madonna	Peter Gabriel	R.E.M.	Aerosmith	Fatboy Slim
20	13	12	10	9

46

Bestselling Kids' Magazine

SEVENTEEN

Two kids' magazines—*Seventeen* and *Highlights*—each sell about 2 million copies per issue. First published in 1944, *Seventeen* is now part of the Hearst Magazine group and is targeted to 14- to 20-year-old girls. It offers teens articles and advice on fashion, beauty, and health, as well as horoscopes and quizzes. *Highlights*, which is geared to a younger audience, was launched in 1946 and offers 5- to 12-year-olds stories, jokes, poems, hidden picture puzzles, and science features.

Bestselling Kids' Magazines

Number of copies
sold per issue, in millions

2.0	2.0	1.3	1.1	1.0
Seventeen	Highlights	National Geographic for Kids	Boys' Life	Sports Illustrated for Kids

Play with the Most Tony Awards

THE PRODUCERS

In March 2001, *The Producers* took home 12 of its record-breaking 15 Tony Award nominations. The Broadway smash won awards for Musical, Original Score, Book, Direction of a Musical, Choreography, Orchestration, Scenic Design, Costume Design, Lighting Design, Actor in a Musical, Featured Actor in a Musical, and Actress in a Musical. *The Producers*, which originally starred Nathan Lane and Matthew Broderick, is a stage adaptation of Mel Brooks's 1968 movie. Brooks wrote the lyrics and music for 16 new songs for the stage version.

Plays with the Most Tony Awards

Awards won

The Producers, 2001	Hello, Dolly! 1964	Spring Awakening, 2007	The Phantom of the Opera, 1988	South Pacific, 2008
12	10	8	7	7

Longest-Running Broadway Show

THE PHANTOM OF THE OPERA

The Phantom of the Opera has been performed more than 8,715 times since it opened in January 1988. The show tells the story of a disfigured musical genius who terrorizes the performers of the Paris Opera House. More than 80 million people have seen a performance, and box-office receipts total more than $3.2 billion. The show won seven Tony Awards its opening year, including Best Musical. The musical drama is performed at the Majestic Theatre.

Longest-Running Broadway Shows
Total performances*

8,715	The Phantom of the Opera, 1988–
7,485	Cats, 1982–2000
6,680	Les Misérables, 1982–2000
6,137	A Chorus Line, 1975–1990
5,959	Oh! Calcutta! 1969–1972

*As of January 15, 2009

49

On the Interstate, 1956–1990

Most-Visited Museum

NATIONAL MUSEUM OF AMERICAN HISTORY

Each year more than 5.8 million visitors pass through the doors of the National Museum of American History in Washington, DC, to learn about America's past. The vast museum has about 3 million artifacts in its collections, which range from Art to Government to Popular Entertainment. The museum, which opened in 1964, measures about 750,000 square feet (69,677 sq m). Some of the more unusual objects housed in the museum include Muhammad Ali's boxing gloves and robe, Evel Knievel's Harley-Davidson, and a Dumbo the Flying Elephant car from the ride in Disneyland.

50

Most-Visited Museums
Annual attendance, in millions

Smithsonian Institution's National Museum of American History, Washington	Smithsonian Institution's National Air and Space Museum, Washington	National Gallery of Art, Washington	Metropolitan Museum of Art, New York	American Museum of Natural History, New York
5.8	5	4.69	4.5	4

SPORTS RECORDS

Basketball • Football
Bicycling • Golf
Baseball • Track and Field
Tennis • Olympics
Figure Skating • Soccer
Car Racing • Motorcycling
Horse Racing • Hockey
X Games • Snowboarding

NBA Team with the Most Championship Titles

BOSTON CELTICS

The Boston Celtics are the most successful team in the NBA with 17 championship wins. The first win came in 1957, and the team went on to win the next 7 consecutive titles—the longest streak of consecutive championship wins in the history of US sports. The most recent championship title came in 2008. The Celtics entered the Basketball Association of America in 1946, which later merged into the NBA in 1949. The Celtics made the NBA play-offs for three consecutive seasons from 2001 to 2004, but they were eliminated in the first round each time.

52

NBA Teams with the Most Championship Titles

Number of championship titles

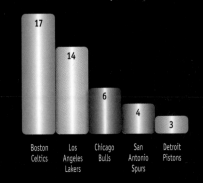

Boston Celtics	Los Angeles Lakers	Chicago Bulls	San Antonio Spurs	Detroit Pistons
17	14	6	4	3

NBA Player with the Highest Career Scoring Average

WILT CHAMBERLAIN & MICHAEL JORDAN

Both Michael Jordan and Wilt Chamberlain averaged an amazing 30.1 points per game during their legendary careers. Jordan played for the Chicago Bulls and the Washington Wizards. He led the league in scoring for seven years. During the 1986 season, he became only the second person ever to score 3,000 points in a single season. Chamberlain played for the Philadelphia Warriors, the Philadelphia 76ers, and the Los Angeles Lakers. In addition to the highest scoring average, he also holds the record for the most games with 50 or more points, with 118.

NBA Players with the Highest Career Scoring Averages

Average points per game

Player	Average
Wilt Chamberlain, 1959–1973	30.1
Michael Jordan, 1984–1998; 2001–2003	30.1
LeBron James, 2003–	27.5
Elgin Baylor, 1958–1971	27.4
Allen Iverson, 1996–	27.1

Michael Jordan

53

NBA's Highest-Scoring Team

DETROIT PISTONS

On December 13, 1983, the Detroit Pistons beat the Denver Nuggets with a score of 186 to 184 at McNichols Arena in Denver, Colorado. The game was tied at 145 at the end of regular play, and three overtime periods were needed to determine the winner. During the game, both the Pistons and the Nuggets each had six players who scored in the double figures. Four players scored more than 40 points each, which was an NBA first. The Pistons scored 74 field goals that night, claiming another NBA record that still stands today.

NBA's Highest-Scoring Teams

Points scored by a team in one game

186	184	173	173	171
Detroit Pistons, vs. Denver Nuggets, 1983	Denver Nuggets, vs. Detroit Pistons, 1983	Boston Celtics, vs. Minneapolis Lakers, 1959	Phoenix Suns, vs. Denver Nuggets, 1990	San Antonio Spurs, vs. Milwaukee Bucks, 1982

NBA Player with the Highest Salary

KEVIN GARNETT

Kevin Garnett earns $24.75 million a season as a forward for the Boston Celtics. Garnett—who stands 1 inch (2.5 cm) shy of 7 feet (2.1 m)—played for the Timberwolves from 1995 to 2007. Since he entered the NBA, he has played in more than 900 games with an average of 20.5 points per game. Garnett also tops the league in rebounds, ranking number one in total rebounds (625), rebounds per game (12.5), defensive rebounds (499), and defensive rebounds per game (10).

NBA Players with the Highest Salaries

Annual salary, in millions of US dollars

Kevin Garnett	Jason Kidd	Jermaine O'Neal	Kobe Bryant	Shaquille O'Neal
24.75	21.37	21.30	21.26	21.00

55

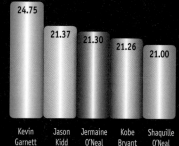

NBA Player with the Most Career Points
KAREEM ABDUL-JABBAR

During his highly successful career, Kareem Abdul-Jabbar scored a total of 38,387 points. In 1969, Abdul-Jabbar began his NBA tenure with the Milwaukee Bucks. He was named Rookie of the Year in 1970. The following year he scored 2,596 points and helped the Bucks win the NBA championship. He was traded to the Los Angeles Lakers in 1975. With his new team, Abdul-Jabbar won the NBA championship in 1980, 1982, 1985, 1987, and 1988. He retired from basketball in 1989 and was inducted into the Basketball Hall of Fame in 1995.

NBA Players with the Most Career Points

Points scored

Kareem Abdul-Jabbar, 1969–1989	Karl Malone, 1985–2004	Michael Jordan, 1984–1998; 2001–2003	Wilt Chamberlain, 1959–1973	Shaquille O'Neal, 1992–
38,387	36,928	32,292	31,419	27,462

WNBA Player with the Highest Free Throw Scoring Average

EVA NEMCOVA & ERICA WHITE

Retired player Eva Nemcova and newcomer Erica White both share the record for the highest free throw average with .897. Nemcova played for the Cleveland Rockets from 1997 to 2001 and was the fourth overall draft pick during the league's inaugural year. White, now a guard for the Indiana Fever, turned pro in 2008. She played previously for the Houston Comets, where she averaged 3.6 points and 1.4 rebounds per game. White was selected as a second-round draft pick after graduating from Louisiana State.

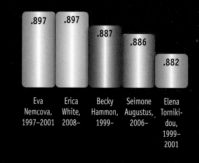

WNBA Players with the Highest Free Throw Scoring Averages

Career free throw average

Eva Nemcova, 1997–2001	Erica White, 2008–	Becky Hammon, 1999–	Seimone Augustus, 2006–	Elena Torniki-dou, 1999–2001
.897	.897	.887	.886	.882

Erica White

WNBA Player with the Highest Career PPG Average

SEIMONE AUGUSTUS

Minnesota Lynx Seimone Augustus leads the WNBA with an average of 21.2 points per game. Augustus was the first overall draft pick in 2006. The 6-foot (1.8 m) guard from Louisiana State was awarded the Naismith Player of the Year Award in 2005, and went on to win the AP Player of the Year Award in 2006. During her first season with the WNBA, Augustus ranked second in points per game (21.9), field goals made (148), points (744), and field goal attempts (620).

58

WNBA Players with the Highest Career PPG Averages

Average points per game*

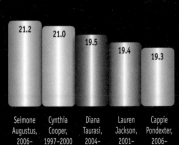

21.2	21.0	19.5	19.4	19.3
Seimone Augustus, 2006–	Cynthia Cooper, 1997–2000	Diana Taurasi, 2004–	Lauren Jackson, 2001–	Cappie Pondexter, 2006–

*As of August 5, 2009

WNBA Player with the Most Career Points

LISA LESLIE

Lisa Leslie—center for the Los Angeles Sparks—has scored 5,909 points in her career. Leslie has a career average of 17.4 points per game. She was named MVP of the WNBA All-Star Games in 1999, 2001, and 2002. Leslie was also a member of the 1996 and 2000 Olympic gold-medal-winning women's basketball teams. In both 2001 and 2002, Leslie led her team to victory in the WNBA championship and was named Finals MVP. Leslie set another record on July 30, 2002, when she became the first player in WNBA history to slam-dunk in a game.

WNBA Players with the Most Career Points

Points scored*

5,909	5,659	5,077	4,945	4,604
Lisa Leslie, 1997–	Tina Thompson, 1997–	Katie Smith, 2000–	Lauren Jackson, 2001–	Sheryl Swoopes, 1997–

*As of August 5, 2009

Women's Basketball Team with the Most NCAA Championships

TENNESSEE

The Tennessee Lady Volunteers have won eight NCAA basketball championships. The Lady Vols won their latest championship in 2008. In 1998, they had a perfect record of 39–0, which was the most seasonal wins ever in women's collegiate basketball. In 2004, Tennessee was in the championship but was beaten by the University of Connecticut Huskies. Since 1976, an impressive 14 Lady Vols have been to the Olympics, and 5 Lady Vols have been inducted into the Women's Basketball Hall of Fame in Knoxville, Tennessee.

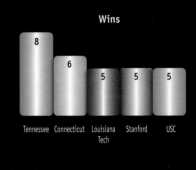

Women's Teams with the Most NCAA Championships

Wins

Tennessee	Connecticut	Louisiana Tech	Stanford	USC
8	6	5	5	5

Men's Basketball Team with the Most NCAA Championships

UCLA

With 11 titles, the University of California, Los Angeles (UCLA) has the most NCAA basketball championship wins. The Bruins won their 11th championship in 1995. The school has won 23 of their last 41 league titles and has been in the NCAA play-offs for 35 of the last 41 years. During the final round of the NCAA championship in 2006, UCLA lost to the Florida Gators with a score of 73 to 57. Not surprisingly, UCLA has produced some basketball legends, including Kareem Abdul-Jabbar, Reggie Miller, and Baron Davis. For the last 36 years, the Bruins have called Pauley Pavilion home.

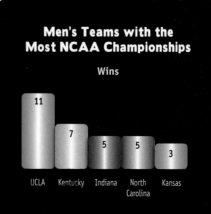

Men's Teams with the Most NCAA Championships

Wins

UCLA	Kentucky	Indiana	North Carolina	Kansas
11	7	5	5	3

NFL Quarterback with the Most Passing Yards

BRETT FAVRE

Quarterback Brett Favre knows how to hit his receivers, completing 65,127 passing yards during his amazing career. He has a completion rate of 61.6 percent, and has connected for 464 touchdowns. Favre is also the NFL's all-time leader in passing touchdowns (464), completions (5,720), and attempts (9,280). Favre began his career with the Atlanta Falcons in 1991. He was traded to the Green Bay Packers the next season, and played for them until 2007. Favre joined the New York Jets in 2008, and retired at the end of the season.

NFL Players with the Most Passing Yards

Yards

Brett Favre, 1991–2009	Dan Marino, 1983–2000	John Elway, 1983–1999	Warren Moon, 1984–2000	Fran Tarkenton, 1961–1978
65,127	61,361	51,475	49,325	47,003

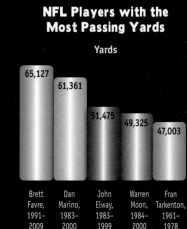

NFL Player with the Highest Career Rushing Total

EMMITT SMITH

Running back Emmitt Smith holds the record for all-time rushing yards with 18,355. Smith began his career with the Dallas Cowboys in 1990 and played with the team until the end of the 2002 season. In 2003, Smith signed a two-year contract with the Arizona Cardinals. Smith also holds the NFL records for the most carries with 4,142 and the most rushing touchdowns with 164. After 15 years in the NFL, Smith retired at the end of the 2004 season.

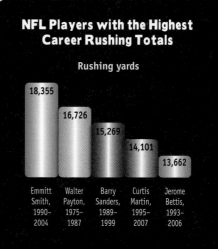

NFL Players with the Highest Career Rushing Totals

Rushing yards

Emmitt Smith, 1990–2004	Walter Payton, 1975–1987	Barry Sanders, 1989–1999	Curtis Martin, 1995–2007	Jerome Bettis, 1993–2006
18,355	16,726	15,269	14,101	13,662

NFL Player with the Most Career Touchdowns

JERRY RICE

Jerry Rice has scored a record 208 touchdowns. He is widely considered to be one of the greatest wide receivers to ever play in the National Football League. Rice holds a total of 14 NFL records, including career receptions (1,549), receiving yards (22,895), receiving touchdowns (197), consecutive 100-catch seasons (4), most games with 100 receiving yards (73), and many others. He was named NFL Player of the Year twice, *Sports Illustrated* Player of the Year four times, and NFL Offensive Player of the Year once. Rice retired from the NFL in 2005.

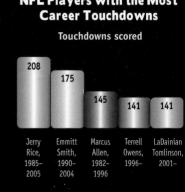

NFL Players with the Most Career Touchdowns

Touchdowns scored

Jerry Rice, 1985–2005	Emmitt Smith, 1990–2004	Marcus Allen, 1982–1996	Terrell Owens, 1996–	LaDainian Tomlinson, 2001–
208	175	145	141	141

NFL Player with the Most Single-Season Touchdowns

LaDAINIAN TOMLINSON

Running back LaDainian Tomlinson scored 31 touchdowns during the 2006 season. He was also named NFL Most Valuable Player that season for his outstanding performance. During his pro career, he has scored a total of 138 touchdowns. Tomlinson was selected fifth overall in the 2001 draft by the San Diego Chargers and continues to play for them today. He holds several team records, including 372 attempts (2002), 100 receptions (2003), and 1,815 rushing yards in a season (2006). Tomlinson has also been named to five Pro Bowls.

NFL Players with the Most Single-Season Touchdowns

Touchdowns scored

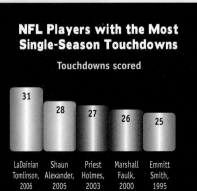

LaDainian Tomlinson, 2006	Shaun Alexander, 2005	Priest Holmes, 2003	Marshall Faulk, 2000	Emmitt Smith, 1995
31	28	27	26	25

NFL Player with the Highest Career Scoring Total

MORTEN ANDERSEN

Morten Andersen leads the NFL in scoring with a career total of 2,544 points. He has made 565 field goals out of 709 attempts, giving him a 79.9 percent completion rate. He has scored 849 extra points out of 859 attempts, resulting in a 98.8 percent success rate. Andersen, a placekicker who began his career in 1982 with the New Orleans Saints, currently plays for the Atlanta Falcons. Known as the Great Dane, partly because of his birthplace of Denmark, Andersen has played 382 professional games. His most successful season was in 1995, when he scored 122 points.

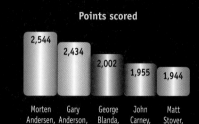

NFL Players with the Highest Career Scoring Totals

Points scored

Morten Andersen, 1982–	Gary Anderson, 1982–2005	George Blanda, 1949–1975	John Carney, 1988–	Matt Stover, 1991–
2,544	2,434	2,002	1,955	1,944

NFL Team with the Most Super Bowl Wins
PITTSBURGH STEELERS

With six championship wins between 1974 and 2009, the Pittsburgh Steelers have won more Super Bowls than any other team in NFL history. The Steelers have also played and won more AFC championship games than any other team in the conference. The Steelers were founded in 1933 and are the fifth-oldest franchise in the league. Twenty-three retired Steelers have been inducted into the Pro Football Hall of Fame, including Franco Harris, Chuck Noll, and Terry Bradshaw.

NFL Teams with the Most Super Bowl Wins

Super Bowls won

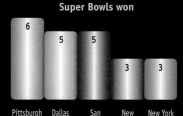

Pittsburgh Steelers	Dallas Cowboys	San Francisco 49ers	New England Patriots	New York Giants
6	5	5	3	3

NFL Coach with the Most Wins

DON SHULA

Don Shula led his teams to a remarkable 347 wins during his 33 years as a head coach in the National Football League. When Shula became head coach of the Baltimore Colts in 1963, he became the youngest head coach in football history. He stayed with the team until 1969 and reached the play-offs 4 times. Shula became the head coach for the Miami Dolphins in 1970 and coached them until 1995. During this time, the Dolphins reached the play-offs 20 times and won at least 10 games a season 21 times. After leading them to Super Bowl wins in 1972 and 1973, Shula became one of only five coaches to win the championship in back-to-back years.

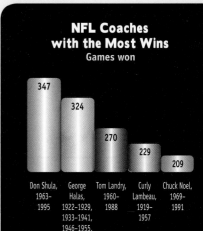

NFL Coaches with the Most Wins
Games won

Coach	Games won
Don Shula, 1963–1995	347
George Halas, 1922–1929, 1933–1941, 1946–1955, 1958–1967	324
Tom Landry, 1960–1988	270
Curly Lambeau, 1919–1957	229
Chuck Noel, 1969–1991	209

NFL's Highest-Paid Player
NNAMDI ASOMUGHA

Oakland Raiders cornerback Nnamdi Asomugha signed a contract worth $28.5 million in 2009. He was a first-round draft pick in 2003, after graduating from the University of California, Berkeley. He was voted Oakland's MVP for the 2006 season and received the team's Commitment to Excellence award. Asomugha was selected as the Raiders' team captain for both the 2007 and 2008 seasons. He was also selected as a starter in the 2009 Pro Bowl. During his six years in the NFL, Asomugha has had 257 tackles.

NFL's Highest-Paid Players

Annual salary, in millions of US dollars

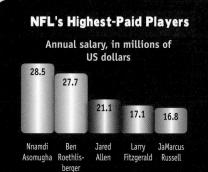

Nnamdi Asomugha	Ben Roethlis-berger	Jared Allen	Larry Fitzgerald	JaMarcus Russell
28.5	27.7	21.1	17.1	16.8

NFL Team with the Most Consecutive Wins

NEW ENGLAND PATRIOTS

Between 2006 and 2007, the New England Patriots won 19 consecutive games. They ended the 2006 regular season with 3 wins. During the 2007 regular season, the team won all 16 games—only the fifth team in league history to do so. During this impressive season, the team set an NFL record by scoring 589 points and 75 touchdowns. The Patriots have a winning history, including 10 AFC East championships, 15 NFL play-off appearances, and 3 Super Bowl wins.

NFL Teams with the Most Consecutive Wins

Consecutive games won

19	18	17	17	16
New England Patriots, 2006–2007	New England Patriots, 2003–2004	Chicago Bears, 1933–1934	Miami Dolphins, 1972–1973	Chicago Bears, 1941–1942

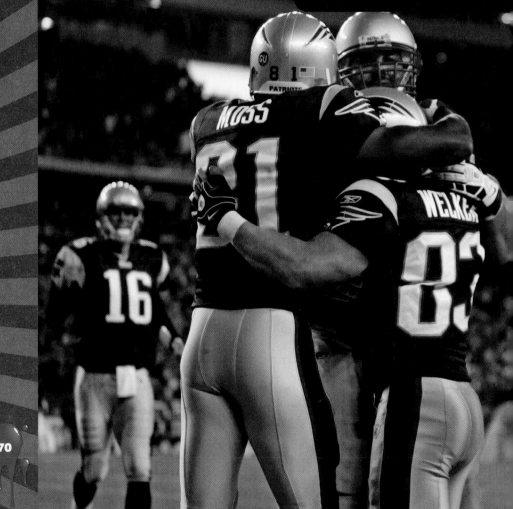

Cyclist with the Most Tour de France Wins
LANCE ARMSTRONG

Lance Armstrong was the first cyclist ever to win seven Tour de France races. He won his first race in 1999, just three years after being diagnosed with cancer. He went on to win the top cycling event for the next six years, retiring after his 2005 victory. Armstrong has received many awards and honors during his career, including being named *Sports Illustrated*'s "Sportsman of the Year" in 2002. Armstrong also formed the Lance Armstrong Foundation, which supports people recovering from cancer.

Cyclists with the Most Tour de France Wins

Number of wins

Lance Armstrong, USA	Eddy Merckx, Belgium	Jacques Anquetil, France	Bernard Hinault, France	Miguel Indurain, Spain
7	5	5	5	5

71

PGA Golfer with the Lowest Seasonal Average

SERGIO GARCIA

Sergio Garcia ruled the course in 2008 with the lowest seasonal average of 69.12. The Spanish golfer turned pro in 1999 and has played in 182 events, making the cut 83 percent of the time. Between 2000 and 2008, Garcia spent more than 250 weeks ranked in the top ten of the Official World Golf Ranking. Garcia has earned more than $24.6 million, ranking 12th on the PGA Tour. He has also won two major awards: the Vardon Trophy and the Byron Nelson Award in 2008.

PGA Golfers with the Lowest Seasonal Averages

Seasonal average in 2008

Sergio Garcia	Phil Mickelson	Padraig Harrington	Anthony Kim	Camilo Villegas
69.12	69.17	69.28	69.28	69.49

LPGA Golfer with the Lowest Seasonal Average

LORENA OCHOA

Lorena Ochoa had the lowest seasonal average in the LPGA in 2008 with 69.70. In fact, that's the fourth-lowest scoring average in LPGA history! Ochoa, who entered the LPGA in 2003, accomplished several impressive feats in 2006. She won six tournaments and was named Rolex Player of the Year. She earned almost $2.6 million, becoming just the second player to pass $2 million in earnings in a single season. During her short career, Ochoa has played in 146 LPGA events and finished in the top three 66 times.

LPGA Golfers with the Lowest Seasonal Averages

Seasonal average in 2008

Lorena Ochoa	Annika Sorenstam	Paula Creamer	Yani Tseng	Cristie Kerr
69.70	70.47	70.56	70.77	70.88

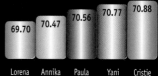

73

LPGA's Highest-Paid Golfer

ANNIKA SORENSTAM

Annika Sorenstam has earned $22.5 million since her LPGA career began in 1994. During this time, she has had 72 career victories, including 9 majors. In 2005, Sorenstam earned her eighth Rolex Player of the Year award—the most in LPGA history. She also became the first player to sweep Rolex Player of the Year honors, the Vare Trophy, and the ADT Official Money List title five times. Sorenstam also earned her fifth consecutive Mizuno Classic title, making her the first golfer in LPGA history to win the same event five consecutive years. Sorenstam retired at the end of the 2008 season.

74

LPGA's Highest-Paid Golfers

Career earnings, in millions of US dollars

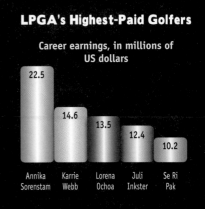

Annika Sorenstam	Karrie Webb	Lorena Ochoa	Juli Inkster	Se Ri Pak
22.5	14.6	13.5	12.4	10.2

Golfer with the Most Major Tournament Wins

JACK NICKLAUS

Golfing great Jack Nicklaus has won a total of 18 major championships. His wins include 6 Masters, 5 PGAs, 4 US Opens, and 3 British Opens. Nicklaus was named PGA Player of the Year five times. He was a member of the winning US Ryder Cup team six times and was an individual World Cup winner a record three times. He was inducted into the World Golf Hall of Fame in 1974, just 12 years after he turned professional. He joined the US Senior PGA Tour in 1990. In addition to playing the game, Nicklaus has designed close to 200 golf courses and written a number of popular books about the sport.

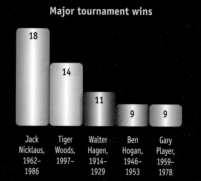

Golfers with the Most Major Tournament Wins

Major tournament wins

18	14	11	9	9
Jack Nicklaus, 1962–1986	Tiger Woods, 1997–	Walter Hagen, 1914–1929	Ben Hogan, 1946–1953	Gary Player, 1959–1978

MLB Player with the Highest Seasonal Home-Run Total

BARRY BONDS

On October 5, 2001, Barry Bonds smashed Mark McGwire's record for seasonal home runs when he hit his 71st home run in the first inning of a game against the Los Angeles Dodgers. In the third inning, he hit number 72, and two days later he reached 73. Bonds, a left fielder for the San Francisco Giants, has a career total of 762 home runs. He also holds the records for seasonal walks (232) and seasonal on-base percentage (.609). Bonds and his father, hitting coach Bobby Bonds, hold the all-time father-son home run record with 1,020.

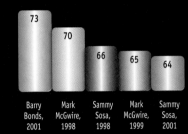

MLB Players with the Highest Seasonal Home-Run Totals

Number of home runs

73	70	66	65	64
Barry Bonds, 2001	Mark McGwire, 1998	Sammy Sosa, 1998	Mark McGwire, 1999	Sammy Sosa, 2001

76

MLB Player with the Most Home Runs
BARRY BONDS

Barry Bonds has hit more home runs than anyone who ever played in the MLB, cracking 762 balls over the wall during his ongoing career. Bonds has hit more than 30 home runs in a season 13 times—another MLB record. During his impressive career, Bonds has won 8 Gold Gloves, 12 Silver Slugger awards, and 13 All-Star awards. Bonds began his career with the Pittsburgh Pirates in 1986; he was transferred to the San Francisco Giants in 1993 and has played for the team since then. He is only one of three players to join the 700 Home Run Club.

MLB Players with the Most Home Runs
Number of home runs*

Barry Bonds, 1986–	Hank Aaron, 1952–1976	Babe Ruth, 1914–1935	Willie Mays, 1948–1973	Ken Griffey, Jr., 1989–
762	755	714	660	622

*As of August 5, 2009

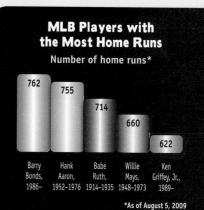

77

MLB Pitcher with the Most Career Strikeouts

NOLAN RYAN

Nolan Ryan leads Major League Baseball with an incredible 5,714 career strikeouts. In his impressive 28-year career, he played for the New York Mets, the California Angels, the Houston Astros, and the Texas Rangers. The right-handed pitcher from Refugio, Texas, led the American League in strikeouts ten times. In 1989, at the age of 42, Ryan became the oldest pitcher ever to lead the Major Leagues in strikeouts. Ryan set another record in 1991 when he pitched his seventh career no-hitter.

MLB Pitchers with the Most Career Strikeouts

Number of strikeouts*

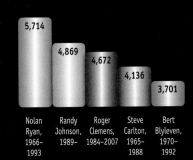

5,714	4,869	4,672	4,136	3,701
Nolan Ryan, 1966–1993	Randy Johnson, 1989–	Roger Clemens, 1984–2007	Steve Carlton, 1965–1988	Bert Blyleven, 1970–1992

*As of August 5, 2009

78

MLB Player with the Most Career Hits

PETE ROSE

Pete Rose belted an amazing 4,256 hits during his 23 years of professional baseball. He got his record-setting hit in 1985, when he was a player-manager for the Cincinnati Reds. By the time Pete Rose retired as a player from Major League Baseball in 1986, he had set several other career records. Rose holds the Major League records for the most career games (3,562), the most times at bat (14,053), and the most seasons with more than 200 hits (10). During his career, he played for the Cincinnati Reds, the Philadelphia Phillies, and the Montreal Expos.

MLB Players with the Most Career Hits

Number of hits

Pete Rose, 1963–1986	Ty Cobb, 1905–1928	Hank Aaron, 1952–1976	Stan Musial, 1941–1963	Tris Speaker, 1907–1928
4,256	4,191	3,771	3,630	3,514

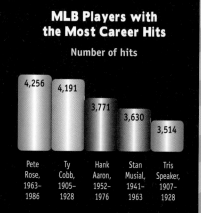

MLB Player with the Most Expensive Contract

ALEX RODRIGUEZ

Alex Rodriguez signed a ten-year deal with the Texas Rangers for $33.0 million in 2001. This does not include any bonuses the shortstop may earn for winning titles or awards, or any money he could make from potential endorsements. The right-hander began his successful career with Seattle in 1994. In 2004, Rodriguez joined the New York Yankees, and that ball club is now responsible for paying the majority of his contract. In 2005, Rodriguez won the American League MVP award.

MLB Players with the Most Expensive Contracts

Yearly salary, in millions of US dollars

33.0	23.9	21.6	20.6	19.2
Alex Rodriguez, New York Yankees	Manny Ramirez, Boston Red Sox	Derek Jeter, New York Yankees	Mark Teixeira, New York Yankees	Carlos Beltran, New York Mets

MLB Player with the Most Career Runs

RICKEY HENDERSON

During his 25 years in the majors, baseball great Rickey Henderson boasts the most career runs with 2,295. Henderson got his start with the Oakland Athletics in 1979, and went on to play for the Yankees, the Mets, the Mariners, the Red Sox, the Padres, the Dodgers, and the Angels. Henderson won a Gold Glove award in 1981, and the American League MVP award in 1989 and 1990. Henderson is also known as the "Man of Steal" because he holds the MLB record for most stolen bases in a career with 1,406.

MLB Players with the Most Career Runs

Number of career runs

Rickey Henderson, 1979–2003	Ty Cobb, 1905–1928	Barry Bonds, 1986–	Hank Aaron, 1954–1976	Babe Ruth, 1914–1935
2,295	2,246	2,227	2,174	2,174

Yogi Berra

Most MVP Awards in the American League

YOGI BERRA, JOE DIMAGGIO, JIMMIE FOXX, MICKEY MANTLE, & ALEX RODRIGUEZ

With three honors each, Yogi Berra, Joe DiMaggio, Jimmie Foxx, Mickey Mantle, and Alex Rodriguez all hold the record for the Most Valuable Player awards during their professional careers. Berra, DiMaggio, Mantle, and Rodriguez were all New York Yankees. Foxx played for the Athletics, the Cubs, and the Phillies. The player with the biggest gap between wins was DiMaggio, who won his first award in 1939 and his last in 1947. Also nicknamed "Joltin' Joe" and the "Yankee Clipper," DiMaggio began playing in the Major Leagues in 1936. The following year, he led the league in home runs and runs scored. He was elected to the Baseball Hall of Fame in 1955.

82

MLB Players with the Most American League MVP Awards

Number of Most Valuable Player (MVP) awards

3	3	3	3	3
Yogi Berra, 1946–1963, 1965	Joe DiMaggio, 1936– 1951	Jimmie Foxx, 1925– 1945	Mickey Mantle, 1951– 1968	Alex Rodriguez, 1994–

Most MVP Awards in the National League
BARRY BONDS

San Francisco Giant Barry Bonds has earned seven Most Valuable Player awards for his amazing achievements in the National League. He received his first two MVP awards in 1990 and 1992 while playing for the Pittsburgh Pirates. The next five awards came while wearing the Giants uniform in 1993, 2001, 2002, 2003, and 2004. Bonds is the first player to win an MVP award three times in consecutive seasons. In fact, Bonds is the only baseball player in history to have won more than three MVP awards.

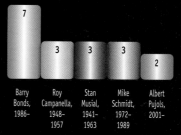

MLB Players with the Most National League MVP Awards

Number of Most Valuable Player (MVP) awards

Player	Awards
Barry Bonds, 1986–	7
Roy Campanella, 1948–1957	3
Stan Musial, 1941–1963	3
Mike Schmidt, 1972–1989	3
Albert Pujols, 2001–	2

MLB Team with the Most World Series Wins

NEW YORK YANKEES

Between 1923 and 2000, the New York Yankees were the World Series champions a record 26 times. The team picked up their latest win in October of 2000 when they beat the New York Mets. The Yankees beat the Mets four games to one to win their third consecutive championship. Since their early days, the team has included some of baseball's greatest players, including Babe Ruth, Lou Gehrig, Yogi Berra, Joe DiMaggio, and Mickey Mantle.

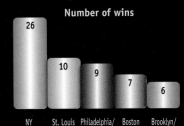

MLB Teams with the Most World Series Wins

Number of wins

NY Yankees	St. Louis Cardinals	Philadelphia/ Kansas City/ Oakland Athletics	Boston Red Sox	Brooklyn/ LA Dodgers
26	10	9	7	6

84

MLB Pitcher with the Most Cy Young Awards
ROGER CLEMENS

Roger Clemens, a starting pitcher for the Houston Astros, has earned a record seven Cy Young Awards during his career so far. He set a Major League record in April 1986 when he struck out 20 batters in one game. He later tied this record in September 1996. In September 2001, Clemens became the first Major League pitcher to win 20 of his first 21 decisions in one season. In June 2003, he became the first pitcher in more than a decade to win his 300th game. He also struck out his 4,000th batter that year.

MLB Pitchers with the Most Cy Young Awards

Number of Cy Young Awards

Roger Clemens, 1984–	Randy Johnson, 1988–	Steve Carlton, 1965–1988	Greg Maddux, 1986–	Pedro Martinez, 1992–
7	5	4	4	3

85

MLB Player with the Most At Bats

PETE ROSE

Pete Rose has stood behind the plate for 14,053 at bats—more than any other Major League player. Rose signed with the Cincinnati Reds after graduating from high school in 1963, and played second base. During his impressive career, Rose set several other records, including the most singles in the Major Leagues (3,315), most seasons with 600 or more at bats in the Major Leagues (17), most career doubles in the National League (746), and most career runs in the National League (2,165). He was also named World Series MVP, *Sports Illustrated* Sportsman of the Year, and *The Sporting News* Man of the Year.

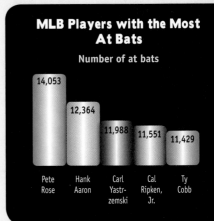

MLB Players with the Most At Bats

Number of at bats

Pete Rose	Hank Aaron	Carl Yastr-zemski	Cal Ripken, Jr.	Ty Cobb
14,053	12,364	11,988	11,551	11,429

MLB Player with the Most Career RBIs

HANK AARON

During his 23 years in the Major Leagues, right-handed Hank Aaron batted in an incredible 2,297 runs. Aaron began his professional career with the Indianapolis Clowns, a team in the Negro American League, in 1952. He was traded to the Milwaukee Braves in 1954 and won the National League batting championship with an average of .328. He was named the league's Most Valuable Player a year later when he led his team to a World Series victory. Aaron retired as a player in 1976 and was inducted into the Baseball Hall of Fame in 1982.

MLB Players with the Most Career RBIs

Number of runs batted in

Hank Aaron, 1952–1976	Babe Ruth, 1914–1935	Cap Anson, 1876–1897	Barry Bonds, 1986–	Lou Gehrig, 1923–1939
2,297	2,217	2,076	1,996	1,995

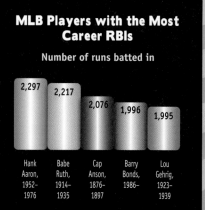

87

MLB Player with the Most Consecutive Games Played

CAL RIPKEN, JR.

Baltimore Oriole Cal Ripken, Jr., played 2,632 consecutive games from May 30, 1982, to September 20, 1998. The right-handed third baseman also holds the record for the most consecutive innings played: 8,243. In June 1996, Ripken broke the world record for consecutive games with 2,216, surpassing Sachio Kinugasa of Japan. When he played as a shortstop, Ripken set Major League records for most home runs (345) and most extra base hits (855) for his position. He started in the All-Star Game a record 19 times in a row.

MLB Players with the Most Consecutive Games Played

Number of consecutive games played

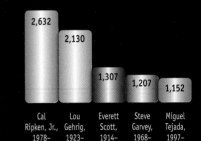

Cal Ripken, Jr., 1978–2001	Lou Gehrig, 1923–1939	Everett Scott, 1914–1925	Steve Garvey, 1968–1988	Miguel Tejada, 1997–
2,632	2,130	1,307	1,207	1,152

Runner with the Fastest Mile
HICHAM EL GUERROUJ

Moroccan runner Hicham El Guerrouj is super speedy—he ran a mile in just over 3 minutes and 43 seconds in July 1999 while racing in Rome. He also holds the record for the fastest mile in North America with a time just short of 3 minutes and 50 seconds. El Guerrouj is an Olympian with gold medals in the 1,500-meter and 5,000-meter races. With this accomplishment at the 2004 Athens games, he became the first runner to win both races at the same Olympics in more than 75 years. El Guerrouj returned to the Olympics in 2006 as a torchbearer in Torino, Italy.

89

Runners with the Fastest Miles
Time, in minutes and seconds

3:43.13	3:43.40	3:44.39	3:44.60	3:44.90
Hicham El Guerrouj, Morocco	Noah Ngeny, Kenya	Noureddine Morceli, Algeria	Hicham El Guerrouj, Morocco	Hicham El Guerrouj, Morocco

World's Top-Earning Female Tennis Player
SERENA WILLIAMS

Serena Williams has earned $23.6 million since she began playing professional tennis in 1995. During her amazing career, Williams has won 28 singles championships and 11 doubles championships, as well as two gold medals in the 2000 and 2008 Olympics. She has also won all four of the Grand Slam championships. Williams has won many impressive awards, including AP's Female Athlete of the Year, the BBC's Sports Personality of the Year, and two Espy Awards.

World's Top-Earning Female Tennis Players
Career earnings, in millions of US dollars

Serena Williams, 1995–	Venus Williams, 1994–	Lindsay Davenport, 1993–	Steffi Graf, 1982–1999	Martina Navratilova, 1975–1994
23.6	22.5	21.9	21.8	21.6

World's Top-Earning Male Tennis Player

ROGER FEDERER

Tennis great Roger Federer has earned more than $45.4 million since his career began in 1998. He has won 57 singles titles and 8 doubles titles, including 15 Grand Slams. His major victories include 3 Australian Opens, 1 French Open, 6 Wimbledon titles, and 5 US Opens. From February 2, 2004, to August 17, 2008, Federer was ranked first in the world for 237 consecutive weeks. He also holds the record for 10 consecutive Grand Slam men's singles finals and 19 consecutive Grand Slam singles semifinals.

World's Top-Earning Male Tennis Players

Career earnings, in millions of US dollars

Roger Federer, 1998–	Pete Sampras, 1990–2003	Andre Agassi, 1986–2006	Boris Becker, 1984–1997	Yevgeny Kafelnikov, 1992–2004
45.4	43.3	31.1	25.1	23.9

91

Woman with the Most Grand Slam Singles Titles

MARGARET COURT SMITH

Margaret Court Smith won 24 Grand Slam singles titles between 1960 and 1975. She is the only woman ever to win the French, British, US, and Australian titles during one year in both the singles and doubles competitions. She was only the second woman to win all four singles titles in the same year. During her amazing career, she won a total of 66 Grand Slam championships—more than any other woman. Court was the world's top-seeded female player from 1962 to 1965, 1969 to 1970, and 1973. She was inducted into the International Tennis Hall of Fame in 1979.

92

Women with the Most Grand Slam Singles Titles

Number of titles won

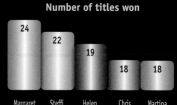

Margaret Court Smith, 1960–1975	Steffi Graf, 1987–1999	Helen Wills-Moody, 1923–1938	Chris Evert-Lloyd, 1974–1986	Martina Navratilova, 1975–1995
24	22	19	18	18

Man with the Most Grand Slam Singles Titles

ROGER FEDERER

Swiss tennis great Roger Federer has won a record 15 Grand Slam championship titles and earned more than $45.4 million since he turned pro in 1998. He has 3 Australian Open wins, 1 French Open win, 6 Wimbledon wins, and 5 US Open wins. Federer is also one of only two players to win the Golden Slam—winning all four Grand Slam championships and an Olympic gold medal in the same year (2008). Federer has a win percentage of 87.5% in major tournaments, and a 94.3% win percentage in singles matches.

Men with the Most Grand Slam Singles Titles

Number of titles won

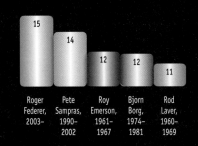

Roger Federer, 2003–	Pete Sampras, 1990–2002	Roy Emerson, 1961–1967	Bjorn Borg, 1974–1981	Rod Laver, 1960–1969
15	14	12	12	11

Country with the Most Summer Olympic Medals

UNITED STATES

94

The United States has won 2,301 medals during the Summer Olympics since officials first began recording the victories in 1896. The medal count breaks down to 932 gold, 730 silver, and 639 bronze. In fact, the United States has more gold medals than the next two highest countries combined. Some summer sports, including men's and women's basketball, have been consistently dominated by Americans throughout the years. The United States also excels in swimming and gymnastics.

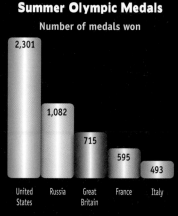

Countries with the Most Summer Olympic Medals

Number of medals won

United States	Russia	Great Britain	France	Italy
2,301	1,082	715	595	493

Country with the Most Winter Olympic Medals
NORWAY

With 280 Olympic medals, Norway leads the world in the winter competition since tallies were first kept in 1924. Norway's medal count consists of 98 gold, 98 silver, and 84 bronze. In fact, several Nordic athletes hold the record for the most medals won in the Winter Olympics—Bjorn Daehlie holds 12 medals in cross country and Ole Einar Bjoerndalen has 9 in the biathlon. The country's chilly climate and mountainous terrain create a perfect place to practice many of the competition's most popular sports, including skiing, bobsled, and snowboarding.

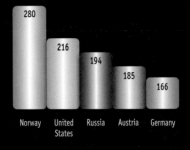

Countries with the Most Winter Olympic Medals
Number of medals won

Norway	United States	Russia	Austria	Germany
280	216	194	185	166

95

Woman with the Most World Figure Skating Championship Wins

SONJA HENIE

Sonja Henie was the queen of the ice, winning ten World Figure Skating Championships between 1927 and 1936. She also won six European Championships during her distinguished career. In addition, Henie won three Olympic gold medals. Born in Norway, Henie was one of the first female skaters to add dance choreography and flashy costumes to her routine. After her final championship in 1936, Henie went to Hollywood and became one of the highest-paid actresses of her time.

Women with the Most World Figure Skating Championship Wins

Number of wins

10	5	5	4	4
Sonja Henie, Norway, 1927–1936	Michelle Kwan, USA, 1996–2003	Herma Szabo, Austria, 1922–1926	Katarina Witt, E. Germany, 1984–1988	Lily Kronberger, Hungary, 1908–1911

Man with the Most World Figure Skating Championship Wins

ULRICH SALCHOW

Swedish figure skater Ulrich Salchow won the World Figure Skating Championships ten times between 1901 and 1911. He also took second place in three other World Championships. Salchow was the first person to land a jump in competition in which he started on the back inside edge of one skate and landed on the back outside edge of the other skate. It was named the Salchow jump in his honor. He also won the first Olympic medal awarded in figure skating when he took the gold at the 1908 games in London.

Men with the Most World Figure Skating Championship Wins

Number of wins

Ulrich Salchow, Sweden, 1901–1911	Karl Schäfer, Austria, 1930–1936	Richard Button, USA, 1948–1952	Kurt Browning, Canada, 1989–1993	Scott Hamilton, USA, 1981–1984
10	7	5	4	4

97

Women's Soccer Team with the Most World Cup Points

USA

The USA women's soccer team has accumulated 14 points during World Cup competition. The Fédération Internationale de Football Association (FIFA) awards 4 points for a win, 3 points for runner-up, 2 points for third place, and 1 point for fourth. The United States won the Cup in 1991 and 1999. They came in third place in 1995, 2003, and 2007. Some of the star players on the US team at the time of these wins included Mia Hamm, Julie Foudy, Brandi Chastain, Kristine Lilly, and Briana Scurry.

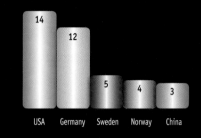

Women's Soccer Teams with the Most World Cup Points

Total number of world Cup points

USA	Germany	Sweden	Norway	China
14	12	5	4	3

Soccer Player with the Highest Salary

DAVID BECKHAM

Each year, soccer superstar David Beckham brings in $42.7 million per year. Beckham normally plays for American Major League Soccer's Los Angeles Galaxy, but he is currently playing for Italy's AC Milan team until the Italian season ends. He also plays on the England national team. With all of this playing time, Beckham became the first British soccer player to compete in 100 Champions League matches. In 2008, he won the Espy Award for Best MLS Player and was inducted into the English Football Hall of Fame.

Soccer Players with the Highest Salaries

Annual salary, in millions of US dollars

David Beckham, LA Galaxy	Lionel Messi, FC Barcelona	Ronaldo, AC Milan	Cristiano Ronaldo, Real Madrid	Thierry Henry, FC Barcelona
42.7	37.7	25.8	24.1	22.4

Woman with the Most CAPS

KRISTINE LILLY

With a total of 340, Kristine Lilly holds the world record for the most CAPS, or international games played. This is the highest number of CAPS in both the men's and women's international soccer organizations. Lilly has played more than 23,500 minutes—that's 392 hours—for the US national team. In 2004, Lilly scored her 100th international goal, becoming one of only five women to ever accomplish that feat. In 2005, Lilly was named US Soccer's Female Athlete of the Year.

Women with the Most CAPS

Number of career CAPS

Kristine Lilly, USA, 1987–	Mia Hamm, USA, 1987–2004	Julie Foudy, USA, 1988–2004	Joy Fawcett, USA, 1987–2004	Tiffeny Milbrett, USA, 1991–2005
340	275	271	239	204

Man with the Most CAPS

MOHAMED AL-DEAYEA

Saudi Arabian soccer great Mohamed Al-Deayea has the most CAPS, or international games, with 181. Al-Deayea began his professional career as a goalie with the Saudi team Al-Ta'ee in 1991 and played there for nine years. In 2000, he became the captain of Al-Hilal. While playing as a part of the Saudi national team, Al-Deayea reached the World Cup three times between 1994 and 2002. He was placed on the 2006 World Cup team but did not play in any games. At the end of the competition, Al-Deayea announced his retirement.

Men with the Most CAPS

Number of career CAPS

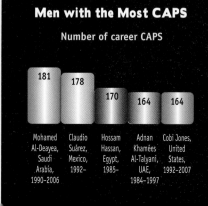

Mohamed Al-Deayea, Saudi Arabia, 1990–2006	Claudio Suárez, Mexico, 1992–	Hossam Hassan, Egypt, 1985–	Adnan Khamées Al-Talyani, UAE, 1984–1997	Cobi Jones, United States, 1992–2007
181	178	170	164	164

Country with the Most World Cup Points

GERMANY

Germany has accumulated a total of 31 points during World Cup soccer competition. A win is worth 4 points, runner-up is worth 3 points, third place is worth 2 points, and fourth place is worth 1 point. Germany won the World Cup four times between 1954 and 1990. Most recently, Germany earned 2 points for a third-place finish in 2006. The World Cup is organized by the Fédération Internationale de Football Association (FIFA) and is played every four years.

Countries with the Most World Cup Points

Total number of points

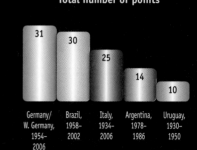

Germany/ W. Germany, 1954– 2006	Brazil, 1958– 2002	Italy, 1934– 2006	Argentina, 1978– 1986	Uruguay, 1930– 1950
31	30	25	14	10

Driver with the Most Formula One Wins
MICHAEL SCHUMACHER

Race-car driver Michael Schumacher won 91 Formula One races in his professional career, which began in 1991. Out of the 250 races he competed in, he reached the podium 154 times. In 2002, Schumacher became the only Formula One driver to have a podium finish in each race in which he competed that season. He won seven world championships between 1994 and 2004. Schumacher, who was born in Germany, began his career with Benetton but later switched to Ferrari. He retired from racing in 2006.

Drivers with the Most Formula One Wins

Number of wins

Driver	Wins
Michael Schumacher	91
Alain Prost	51
Ayrton Senna	41
Nigel Mansell	31
Jackie Stewart	27

103

104

Driver with the Fastest Daytona 500 Win

BUDDY BAKER

Race-car legend Buddy Baker dominated the competition at the 1980 Daytona 500 with an average speed of over 177 miles (285 km) per hour. It was the first Daytona 500 race run under three hours. Baker had a history of speed before this race—he became the first driver to race more than 200 miles (322 km) per hour on a closed course in 1970. During his amazing career, Baker competed in 688 Winston Cup races—he won 19 of them and finished in the top five in 198 others. He also won more than $3.6 million. He was inducted into the International Motorsports Hall of Fame in 1997.

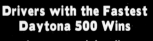

Drivers with the Fastest Daytona 500 Wins

Average speed, in miles (kilometers) per hour

177.60 (285.82)	176.26 (283.66)	172.71 (277.95)	172.26 (277.23)	169.65 (273.03)
Buddy Baker, 1980	Bill Elliott, 1987	Dale Earnhardt, 1998	Bill Elliott, 1985	Richard Petty, 1981

Driver with the Fastest Indianapolis 500 Win
ARIE LUYENDYK

In 1990, race-car driver Arie Luyendyk won the Indianapolis 500 with an average speed of almost 186 miles (299 km) per hour—the fastest average speed ever recorded in the history of the race. This was the first Indy 500 race for Luyendyk, and he drove a Lola/Chevy Indy V8 as part of the Shierson Racing team. In 1997, Luyendyk had another Indy 500 victory with an average speed of 146 miles (235 km) per hour. He also holds the record for the fastest Indy 500 practice lap at a speed of 239 miles (385 km) per hour.

Drivers with the Fastest Indianapolis 500 Wins

Average speed, in miles (kilometers) per hour

Arie Luyendyk, 1990	Rick Mears, 1991	Bobby Rahal, 1986	Juan-Pablo Montoya, 2000	Emerson Fittipaldi, 1989
185.98 (299.30)	176.45 (283.98)	170.72 (274.75)	167.61 (269.73)	167.58 (269.73)

NASCAR Driver with the Highest Career Earnings

JEFF GORDON

Jeff Gordon has earned more than $76 million since he began racing in 1991. In fact, he was the first driver in history to earn more than $50 million. To date, Gordon has won 4 Winston Cup titles, 3 Daytona 500 titles, and 73 NASCAR Cup victories. His first Daytona 500 win in 1997 came when he was just 25 years old, making him the race's youngest winner. Gordon has 81 career NASCAR victories, placing him sixth on the all-time wins list. He has raced for Hendrick Motorsports since 1992, and is part owner in the business.

106

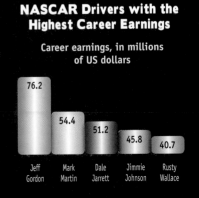

NASCAR Drivers with the Highest Career Earnings

Career earnings, in millions of US dollars

Jeff Gordon	Mark Martin	Dale Jarrett	Jimmie Johnson	Rusty Wallace
76.2	54.4	51.2	45.8	40.7

Rider with the Most Superbike Race Wins
CARL FOGARTY

UK driver Carl Fogarty won 59 Superbike races during his career. Known by the nickname "Foggy" to his fans, Fogarty won the World Superbike Championship in 1994, 1995, 1998, and 1999. As part of the Ducati racing team, Fogarty set a lap record at the Isle of Man TT Race after he clocked 18 minutes and 18 seconds on a Yamaha 750cc in 1992. He also competed in the 1995 Daytona 200 and finished second. Fogarty retired from racing in 2000.

Riders with the Most Superbike Race Wins

Number of races won

Carl Fogarty, UK	Troy Corser, Australia	Colin Edwards, USA	Doug Polen, USA	Raymond Roche, France
59	33	31	27	23

Rider with the Most Motocross World Titles

STEFAN EVERTS

Stefan Everts is the king of Motocross with a total of ten world titles. He won twice on a 500cc bike, seven more times on a 250cc bike, and once on a 125cc bike. During his 18-year career, he had 101 Grand Prix victories. Everts was named Belgium Sportsman of the Year five times. He retired after his final world title in 2006 and is now a consultant and coach for the riders who compete for the KTM racing team.

108

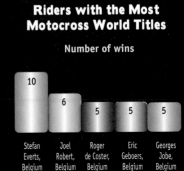

Riders with the Most Motocross World Titles

Number of wins

10	6	5	5	5
Stefan Everts, Belgium	Joel Robert, Belgium	Roger de Coster, Belgium	Eric Geboers, Belgium	Georges Jobe, Belgium

Jockey with the Most Triple Crown Wins

EDDIE ARCARO

Between 1938 and 1961, jockey Eddie Arcaro won a total of 17 Triple Crown races. Nicknamed "the Master," Arcaro won the Kentucky Derby five times, the Preakness six times, and the Belmont six times. He holds the record for the most Preakness wins, and is tied for the most Kentucky Derby and Belmont wins. He was also horse racing's top money winner six times between 1940 and 1955. During his career, Arcaro competed in 24,092 races and won 4,779 of them.

Jockeys with the Most Triple Crown Wins

Number of wins

Eddie Arcaro	Bill Shoemaker	Bill Hartack	Earl Sande	Pat Day
17	11	9	9	9

NHL Team with the Most Stanley Cup Wins

MONTREAL CANADIENS

The Montreal Canadiens won an amazing 24 Stanley Cup victories between 1916 and 1993. That's almost one-quarter of all the Stanley Cup championships ever played. The team plays at Montreal's Molson Centre. The Canadiens were created in December 1909 by J. Ambrose O'Brien to play for the National Hockey Association (NHA). They eventually made the transition into the National Hockey League. Over the years, the Canadiens have included such great players as Maurice Richard, George Hainsworth, Jacques Lemaire, Saku Koivu, and Emile Bouchard.

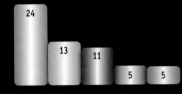

NHL Teams with the Most Stanley Cup Wins

Number of Stanley Cups wins

Montreal Canadiens	Toronto Maple Leafs	Detroit Red Wings	Boston Bruins	Edmonton Oilers
24	13	11	5	5

NHL Player with the Most Career Points

WAYNE GRETZKY

Wayne Gretzky scored an unbelievable 2,857 points and 894 goals during his 20-year career. Gretzky was the first person in the NHL to average more than two points per game. Many people consider Canadian-born Gretzky to be the greatest player in the history of the National Hockey League. In fact, he is called "the Great One." He officially retired from the sport in 1999 and was inducted into the Hockey Hall of Fame that same year. After his final game, the NHL retired his jersey number (99). In 2005, Gretzky became the head coach of the Phoenix Coyotes.

NHL Players with the Most Career Points

Number of points scored

Wayne Gretzky, 1979–1999	Mark Messier, 1979–2004	Gordie Howe, 1954–1980	Ron Francis, 1981–2004	Marcel Dionne, 1971–1990
2,857	1,887	1,850	1,798	1,771

111

NHL Goalie with the Most Career Wins

MARTIN BRODEUR

Not much gets by goalie Martin Brodeur—he's won 553 games since he was drafted by the New Jersey Devils in 1990. Still with the Devils, Brodeur has helped the team win three Stanley Cup championships. He is also the only goalie in NHL history to complete seven seasons with 40 or more wins. Brodeur has been an NHL All-Star ten times, and has received the Vezina Trophy and the Jennings Trophy four times each. He also ranks second in the league in regular-season shutouts.

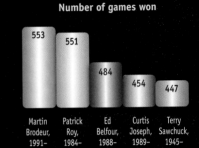

NHL Goalies with the Most Career Wins

Number of games won

Martin Brodeur, 1991–	Patrick Roy, 1984–2003	Ed Belfour, 1988–	Curtis Joseph, 1989–	Terry Sawchuck, 1945–1970
553	551	484	454	447

Most Valuable Hockey Team

TORONTO MAPLE LEAFS

The Toronto Maple Leafs are worth an astounding $448 million, making them the most valuable hockey team in the world. This value is determined by assigning a monetary value to each of the team's players, based on their skills, performance, and contract value. Formerly known as the Toronto Arenas, the team was formed in 1917. Ten years later, the team changed to its current name. The Leafs won 13 Stanley Cups between 1918 and 1967. Some of the most famous players associated with the team include Turk Broda, Tim Horton, Syl Apps, Darryl Sittler, and Ed Belfour. The team's home ice is at the Air Canada Centre.

Most Valuable Hockey Teams

Team value, in millions of US dollars

Team	Value
Toronto Maple Leafs	448
New York Rangers	411
Montreal Canadiens	334
Detroit Red Wings	303
Philadelphia Flyers	275

Skateboarder with the Most X Game Gold Medals

TONY HAWK

American Tony Hawk won ten gold medals for skateboarding in the Extreme Games between 1995 and 2002. All his medals came in vertical competition, meaning that the riders compete on a vert ramp similar to a half-pipe. Hawk is most famous for nailing the 900—completing 2.5 rotations in the air before landing back on the ramp. He has also invented many skateboarding tricks, including the McHawk, the Madonna, and the Stalefish. Although Hawk is retired from professional skateboarding, he is still active in several businesses, including video game consulting, film production, and clothing design.

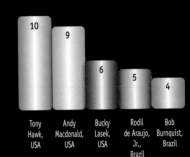

Skateboarders with the Most X Game Gold Medals

Number of gold medals won

Tony Hawk, USA	Andy Macdonald, USA	Bucky Lasek, USA	Rodil de Araujo, Jr., Brazil	Bob Burnquist, Brazil
10	9	6	5	4

Athlete with the Most X Game Medals

DAVE MIRRA

Dave Mirra has won 20 medals—14 gold, 4 silver, and 2 bronze—in X Game competition. He has medaled in every X Game since he entered the games in 1995. All of Mirra's medals have come in BMX competition, where he performs tricks such as double backflips, frontflips, triple tailwhips, and backflip drop-ins. In 2006, Mirra formed his own bike company named MirraCo, and he now competes for the company with other top BMX riders. That same year also marked Mirra's first absence from the X Games because of injury.

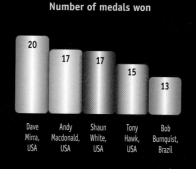

Athletes with the Most X Game Medals

Number of medals won

Dave Mirra, USA	Andy Macdonald, USA	Shaun White, USA	Tony Hawk, USA	Bob Burnquist, Brazil
20	17	17	15	13

115

Snowboarder with the Most World Championship Medals

NICOLAS HUET

Nicolas Huet has won five championship medals while competing as a snowboarder with the Fédération Internationale de Ski (FIS). Huet's medals include two golds, one silver, and two bronzes. Huet's first medal came in 1999 when he won gold in Germany, and his most recent medals came in 2005 when he won a silver and a bronze in Canada. His medals were earned on the parallel slalom and the parallel giant slalom. Nicknamed Nico, Huet spends his time golfing and surfing when he's not on the slopes.

116

Snowboarders with the Most World Championship Medals

Number of medals won

Nicolas Huet, France	Antti Autti, Finland	Jasey-Jay Anderson, Canada	Mike Jacoby, USA	Helmut Pramstaller, Austria
5	4	4	3	3

SCIENCE RECORDS

Video Games
Internet
Computers
Vehicles
Technology

World's Bestselling Video Game

WII SPORTS

Nintendo's Wii Sports is the bestselling video game in history, with more than 41.6 million copies sold around the globe. One reason the game is so widespread is that it has come packaged with the Wii console since the system debuted in November 2006. In Japan, however, the game is not included with the console, and it sold 176,167 copies on its day of release. Wii Sports features five games: bowling, golf, baseball, tennis, and boxing. Players use special motion-sensor remotes that are recognized by the console to act out the different movements required for each game.

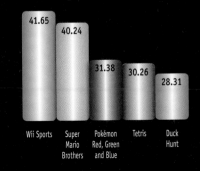

World's Bestselling Video Games

Number of copies sold, in millions

Wii Sports	Super Mario Brothers	Pokémon Red, Green and Blue	Tetris	Duck Hunt
41.65	40.24	31.38	30.26	28.31

World's Bestselling Video Game Genre
ACTION

When it comes to video games, people like action! More than 22 percent of all video games sold come from the action category. Action games often require players to use quick reflexes to battle opponents and overcome obstacles. Many of these games also allow players to move up to a new level of play once one is complete. Other action games—such as the top-selling Super Mario Bros. series—are based on a quest to save a princess or find a treasure. Some other types of action games include fighting games and arcade games.

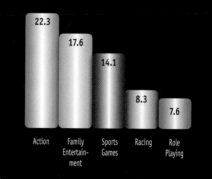

World's Bestselling Video Game Genres

Percent of all video games sold

Action	Family Entertainment	Sports Games	Racing	Role Playing
22.3	17.6	14.1	8.3	7.6

World's Most-Visited Web Site

GOOGLE

The Web search engine Google has 144.2 million unique users each month. That's the equivalent of half the United States' population logging on to the site! Google is the world's largest online index of Web sites. In addition, Google offers e-mail, maps, news, and finance sites. Google was founded in 1998 by Stanford University students Larry Page and Sergey Brin. A "googol" is a 1 followed by 100 zeros, and the site was named after the term to show that its mission was to organize the virtually infinite amount of information on the Web.

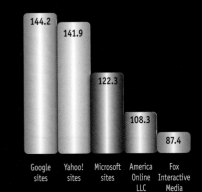

World's Most-Visited Web Sites

Number of unique users each month, in millions

Google sites	Yahoo! sites	Microsoft sites	America Online LLC	Fox Interactive Media
144.2	141.9	122.3	108.3	87.4

World's Most-Visited Shopping Site

EBAY

When online shoppers are looking to spend money, the majority check eBay first. With 69.3 million visitors each month, eBay truly is the World's Online Marketplace. The company was founded in 1995, and the online auction and shopping Web site attracts sellers and bidders from all over the world. Each year, millions of items—including spectacular treasures, unusual services, and even worthless junk—trade hands. Some of the most expensive sales include a Grumman Gulfstream II jet for $4.9 million and a 1909 Honus Wagner baseball card for $1.65 million.

World's Most-Visited Shopping Sites

Number of unique users each month, in millions

eBay.com	Amazon.com	Apple.com	Craigslist.com	Target.com
69.3	55.7	47.5	35.2	32.1

121

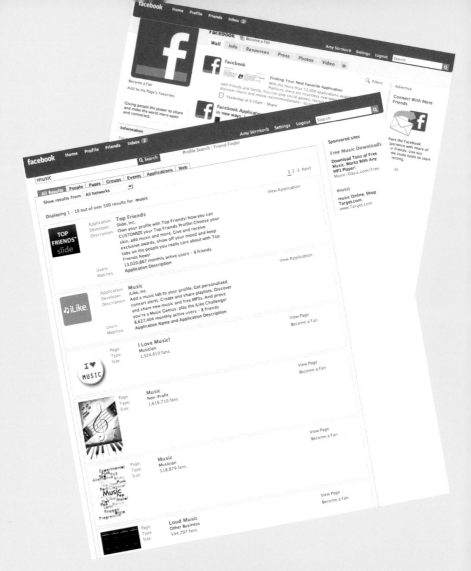

Most-Visited Social Network Site

FACEBOOK

The social site Facebook has almost 1.2 billion hits per month, and 68.5 million of those hits are unique visitors. Facebook was created by Mark Zuckerberg in 2004 as a network site for Harvard University students to chat with each other, send messages, and post updates on their walls. It was a huge hit, and more than 30 other universities were up and running within four months. In 2007, Facebook took off with mainstream users and was signing up about 1 million new users a week. Today, most users sign on every day, and spend an average of 19 minutes a day socializing.

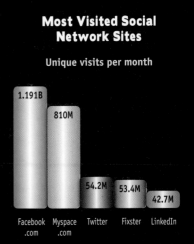

Most Visited Social Network Sites

Unique visits per month

Facebook.com	Myspace.com	Twitter	Fixster	LinkedIn
1.191B	810M	54.2M	53.4M	42.7M

122

Most-Visited Newspaper Web Site
NYTIMES.COM

Each month, approximately 18.2 million people log on to check out the latest happenings around the world on the New York Times Web site. The site offers everything found in the print addition, including U.S. and world news, sports, science, arts, travel, and classified sections. The online readers for the Times increased about 6 percent from the previous year, and online newspapers in general increased readership by about 27 percent. Because internet access is so readily available at home, work, schools, libraries, and even phones, online news is often faster and easier to obtain than the written version.

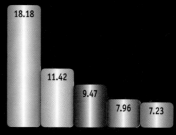

Most Visited Web Sites

Average hits per month, in millions

18.18	11.42	9.47	7.96	7.23
Nytimes .com	Usatoday .com	Washing- tonpost .com	Latimes .com	Wall Street Journal Online

World's Most-Used E-mail Service

YAHOO! MAIL

Yahoo! Mail has almost 88,000 new visitors each month—more than the next two most popular e-mail services combined. Yahoo! Mail has more than 260 million users worldwide. Some popular features that the e-mail service includes are unlimited e-mail storage, instant and text messaging from mailboxes, and advanced protection from spam and viruses. The mail service, which is part of the bigger Yahoo! company, began in 1996. Founders David Filo and Jerry Yang created Yahoo! while they were students at Stanford University.

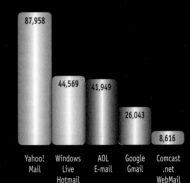

World's Most-Used E-mail Service

Number of new users per month

Yahoo! Mail	Windows Live Hotmail	AOL E-mail	Google Gmail	Comcast .net WebMail
87,958	44,569	41,949	26,043	8,616

Country with the Most Web Sites

UNITED STATES

The United States has the most sites on the World Wide Web with 316 million. That's more than half of the 556 million Web sites worldwide that make up the Internet today. There are currently more than 5,000 times more Web sites running today than were on the Web just ten years ago. Web site production has increased at this incredible rate because sites have become so much easier to create. Bloggers and small business owners account for the largest percentage of new Web sites.

Countries with the Most Web Sites

Number of Web sites, in millions

USA	Japan	Germany	Italy	China
316.0	39.9	22.6	17.7	14.3

Country with the Highest Internet Usage

ICELAND

Iceland has the world's highest percentage of Internet users, with 90 percent of the country logging on to surf the Web. That means about 273,900 people in the small European country have Internet access, and 97,900 are broadband subscribers. In comparison, only about 48.5 percent of the population in Europe as a whole goes online. Icelandic people mainly use the Internet to find information and to communicate, with about 36 percent of users also shopping online. Iceland has about 20 Internet providers, and subscribers pay approximately $60 a month for service.

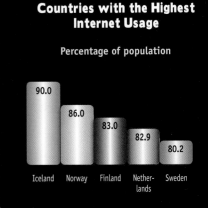

Countries with the Highest Internet Usage

Percentage of population

Iceland	Norway	Finland	Nether-lands	Sweden
90.0	86.0	83.0	82.9	80.2

Country with the Most Internet Users

UNITED STATES

The number of Internet users has more than doubled in the last five years. Americans now account for 17 percent of users worldwide. In the United States, more than 222 million people are surfing the World Wide Web. That's more than 50 percent of the population. Throughout the nation, the largest number of Internet users are women between the ages of 18 and 54, closely followed by men in that age group. Teens ages 12 to 17 are the third-largest Internet-using group. The average Internet user spends about 14 hours online per week.

Countries with the Most Internet Users

Users, in millions

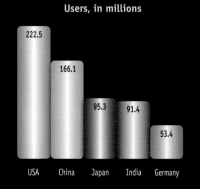

USA	China	Japan	India	Germany
222.5	166.1	95.3	91.4	53.4

Country with the Most Personal Computers

UNITED STATES

Throughout the United States, there are a total of 274.1 million personal computers in use. This is more than 22 percent of the world's total personal computer usage. In 2008, 86 percent of the population used a personal computer. It's estimated that the United States will have more computers in use than it will have people by 2013. The United States is one of only two countries that has more PCs in use than it has cell phone subscribers. The total number of personal computers in use worldwide totals 1.2 billion units.

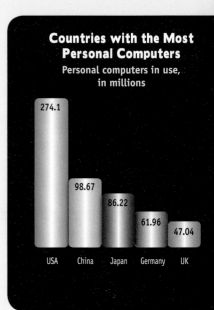

Countries with the Most Personal Computers
Personal computers in use, in millions

USA	China	Japan	Germany	UK
274.1	98.67	86.22	61.96	47.04

World's Fastest Passenger Train

MAGLEV

The superspeedy MagLev train in China carries passengers from Pudong financial district to Pudong International Airport at an average speed of 267 miles (427 km) per hour. The 8-minute train ride replaces a 45-minute car trip. A one-way ticket costs about $7.30. The MagLev, which is short for "magnetic levitation," actually floats in the air just above the track. Tiny magnets are used to suspend the train, and larger ones are used to pull it forward. The German-built train began commercial operation in 2004.

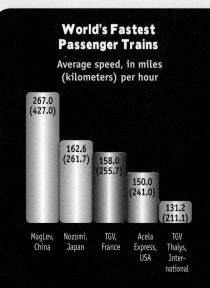

World's Fastest Passenger Trains

Average speed, in miles (kilometers) per hour

MagLev, China	Nozomi, Japan	TGV, France	Acela Express, USA	TGV Thalys, International
267.0 (427.0)	162.6 (261.7)	158.0 (255.7)	150.0 (241.0)	131.2 (211.1)

World's Smallest Car
PEEL P50

The Peel P50 is the smallest production car ever made, measuring just 4.25 feet (1.3 m) long. That's not much longer than the average adult bicycle! The Peel P50 was produced in the Isle of Man between 1962 and 1965, and only 46 cars were made. It is just big enough to hold one adult and one bag. The Peel P50 has three wheels, one door, one windshield wiper, and one headlight, and was available in red, white, or blue. The microcar weighs just 130 pounds (58.9 kg) and measures about 4 feet (1.2 m) tall. With its three-speed manual transmission, it can reach a top speed of 38 miles (61 km) an hour. However, it cannot go in reverse.

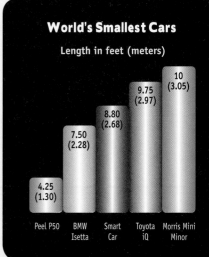

World's Smallest Cars

Length in feet (meters)

Peel P50	BMW Isetta	Smart Car	Toyota iQ	Morris Mini Minor
4.25 (1.30)	7.50 (2.28)	8.80 (2.68)	9.75 (2.97)	10 (3.05)

World's Fastest Land Vehicle

THRUST SSC

The Thrust SSC, which stands for Supersonic Car, reached a speed of 763 miles (1,228 km) per hour on October 15, 1997. At that speed, a car could make it from San Francisco to New York City in less than four hours. The Thrust SSC is propelled by two jet engines capable of 110,000 horsepower. It has the same power as 1,000 Ford Escorts or 145 Formula One race cars. The Thrust SSC runs on jet fuel, using about five gallons (19 L) per second. It only takes approximately five seconds for this supersonic car to reach its top speed. It is 54 feet (16.5 m) long and weighs seven tons (6.4 t).

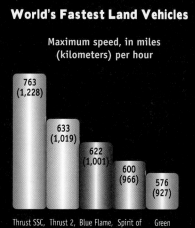

World's Fastest Land Vehicles

Maximum speed, in miles (kilometers) per hour

763 (1,228)	Thrust SSC 1997
633 (1,019)	Thrust 2 1983
622 (1,001)	Blue Flame 1970
600 (966)	Spirit of America, 1965
576 (927)	Green Monster, 1965

World's Fastest Production Car

SSC ULTIMATE AERO

The superspeedy SSC Ultimate Aero can reach a top speed of 257 miles (414 km) per hour! At that rate, person could drive from Boston to Los Angeles in just 11.5 hours. The Aero can accelerate from 0 to 60 miles per hour in just 2.78 seconds, and cover a quarter mile in just 9.9 seconds. The Aero is powered by a twin turbo V-8 engine producing 1,183 horsepower. The SSC Ultimate Aero is built by Shelby Super Cars, and the design took seven years to perfect.

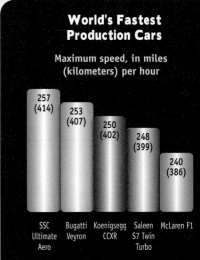

World's Fastest Production Cars

Maximum speed, in miles (kilometers) per hour

SSC Ultimate Aero	Bugatti Veyron	Koenigsegg CCXR	Saleen S7 Twin Turbo	McLaren F1
257 (414)	253 (407)	250 (402)	248 (399)	240 (386)

World's Biggest Monster Truck

BIGFOOT 5

The Bigfoot 5 truly is a monster—it measures 15.4 feet (4.7 m) high! That's about three times the height of an average car. Bigfoot 5 has 10-foot (3 m) Firestone Tundra tires, each weighing 2,400 pounds (1,088 kg), giving the truck a total weight of about 38,000 pounds (17,236 kg). The giant wheels were from an arctic snow train operated in Alaska by the US Army in the 1950s. This modified 1996 Ford F250 pickup truck is owned by Bob Chandler of St. Louis, Missouri. The great weight of this monster truck makes it too large to race.

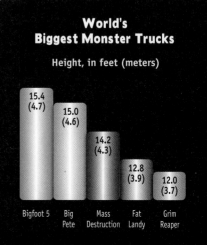

World's Biggest Monster Trucks

Height, in feet (meters)

15.4 (4.7)	15.0 (4.6)	14.2 (4.3)	12.8 (3.9)	12.0 (3.7)
Bigfoot 5	Big Pete	Mass Destruction	Fat Landy	Grim Reaper

133

World's Largest Cruise Ship

OASIS OF THE SEAS

Royal Caribbean's latest cruise ship—the *Oasis of the Seas*—weighs in at an incredible 220,000 gross tons (199,580 t). The ship is more like a floating city with seven different neighborhoods: Central Park, Boardwalk, Royal Promenade, the Pool and Sports Zone, Vitality at Sea Spa and Fitness Center, Entertainment Place, and Youth Zone. *Oasis of the Seas*, which measures 16 decks high, also includes more than 20 different eateries, 3 pools, a water park, and a zip-line ride. The giant ship boasts 2,700 staterooms and can accommodate 5,400 guests.

World's Largest Cruise Ships

Weight, in gross tons (tonnes)

222,000 (199,580)	160,000 (145,600)	160,000 (145,600)	160,000 (145,600)	151,400 (137,350)
Oasis of the Seas	Freedom of the Seas	Independence of the Seas	Liberty of the Seas	Queen Mary 2

World's Fastest Plane

X-43A

NASA's experimental X-43A plane reached a top speed of Mach 9.8—or more than nine times the speed of sound—on a test flight over the Pacific Ocean in November 2004. The X-43A was mounted on top of a Pegasus rocket booster and was carried into the sky by a B-52 aircraft. The booster was then fired, taking the X-43A about 110,000 feet (33,530 m) above the ground. The rocket was detached from the unmanned X-43A, and the plane flew unassisted for several minutes. At this rate of 7,459 miles (12,004 km) per hour, a plane could circle Earth in just over three and a half hours!

World's Fastest Planes

Maximum speed, in miles (kilometers) per hour

Plane	Speed
X-43A	7,459 (12,004)
X-15	5,115 (8,232)
Lockheed SR-71 Blackbird	2,436 (3,920)
MiG-25R Foxbat-B	2,436 (3,920)
X-2	2,436 (3,920)

World's Lightest Jet

BD-5J MICROJET

The BD-5J Microjet weighs only 358.8 pounds (162.7 kg), making it the lightest jet in the world. At only 12 feet (3.7 m) in length, it is one of the smallest as well. This tiny jet has a height of 5.6 feet (1.7 m) and a wingspan of 17 feet (5.2 m). The Microjet uses a TRS-18 turbojet engine. It can reach a top speed of 320 miles (514.9 km) per hour, but can only carry 32 gallons (121 L) of fuel at a time. A new BD-5J costs around $200,000. This high-tech gadget was flown by James Bond in the movie *Octopussy*, and it is also occasionally used by the US military.

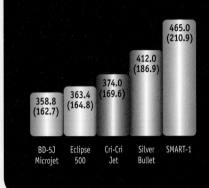

World's Lightest Jets
Weight, in pounds (kilograms)

BD-5J Microjet	Eclipse 500	Cri-Cri Jet	Silver Bullet	SMART-1
358.8 (162.7)	363.4 (164.8)	374.0 (169.6)	412.0 (186.9)	465.0 (210.9)

World's Fastest Helicopter
V-22 OSPREY

The Bell Boeing V-22 Osprey can reach a top speed of 316 miles (509 kilometers) per hour. The Osprey has rotors that allow it to take off and land like a helicopter, but once it's airborne, its engine can rotate to turn the aircraft into a turboprop airplane. This makes the Osprey ideal for several different types of military missions, including combat support, long-range special ops, and search and rescue. The Osprey can carry 24 combat troops, as well as 20,000 pounds (9071 kg) of interior cargo or 15,000 pounds (6803 kg) of external cargo.

World's Fastest Helicopters

Top speed, in miles (kilometers) per hour

V-22 Osprey	Sikorsky X-2	G-LYNX	Sikorsky S76C	Eurocopter EC155 B1
316 (509)	287 (462)	249 (401)	177 (285)	170 (274)

137

Suzuki GSX1300R
Hayabusa

World's Fastest Production Motorcycle
SUZUKI GSX1300R HAYABUSA & KAWASAKI NINJA ZX-14

Both the Suzuki GSX1300R Hayabusa and the Kawasaki Ninja ZX-14 are capable of reaching a top speed of 186 miles (299 km) per hour. That's three times faster than the speed limit on most major highways. The Hayabusa, which is named after one of the world's fastest birds, features a 1299cc, liquid-cooled DOHC engine. The Ninja ZX-14 has a 1352cc four-stroke engine and can go from 0 to 60 miles per hour in just 2.5 seconds. In 2001, motorcycle manufacturers set a guideline stating that no new production motorcycles will have a top speed above 186 miles (299 km) per hour, for safety reasons.

138

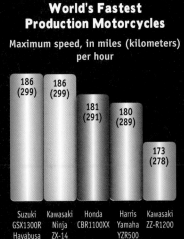

World's Fastest Production Motorcycles

Maximum speed, in miles (kilometers) per hour

Suzuki GSX1300R Hayabusa	Kawasaki Ninja ZX-14	Honda CBR1100XX	Harris Yamaha YZR500	Kawasaki ZZ-R1200
186 (299)	186 (299)	181 (291)	180 (289)	173 (278)

World's Tallest Roller Coaster
KINGDA KA

Kingda Ka towers over Six Flags Great Adventure in Jackson, New Jersey, at a height of 456 feet (139 m). Its highest drop plummets riders down 418 feet (127 m). The steel coaster can reach a top speed of 128 miles (206 km) per hour in just 3.5 seconds, and it was the fastest coaster in the world when it opened in 2005. The entire 3,118-foot (950 m) ride is over in just 28 seconds. The hydraulic launch coaster is located in the Golden Kingdom section of the park. It can accommodate about 1,400 riders per hour.

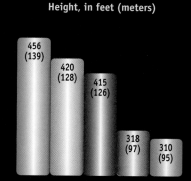

World's Tallest Roller Coasters

Height, in feet (meters)

Kingda Ka, USA	Top Thrill Dragster, USA	Superman: The Escape, USA	Steel Dragon 2000, Japan	Millennium Force, USA
456 (139)	420 (128)	415 (126)	318 (97)	310 (95)

World's Bestselling Cell Phone Company

NOKIA

Nokia has sold more than 481 million cell phones worldwide—about 37 percent of the global mobile phone market share. Nokia launched its first mobile phones in the late 1980s, and each weighed about 11 pounds (4.9 kg). Today Nokia features many much sleeker models, which offer the latest in texting, e-mail, gaming, and music. The giant multinational communications company is based in Finland and sells products in more than 150 countries. Nokia is the fifth most valuable global brand, with a worth of $35.9 billion.

140

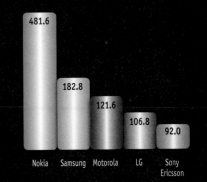

World's Bestselling Cell Phone Companies

Number of cell phones sold, in millions

Nokia	Samsung	Motorola	LG	Sony Ericsson
481.6	182.8	121.6	106.8	92.0

Country with the Most Cell Phone Accounts
ITALY

There are more than 135 cell phone accounts for every 100 people in Italy. This means that many of the country's residents have two or more accounts. Cell phones are so popular in Italy because they are often cheaper than traditional landlines. The largest cell phone provider is Telcom Italia Mobil SpA, with 25 million subscribers. The company introduced an extremely popular service that lets subscribers watch soccer video highlights on their phones and send clips and messages to friends. In the first month this service was available, more than 500,000 messages were sent.

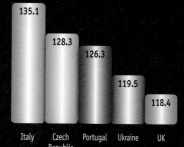

Countries with the Most Cell Phone Accounts

Cell phone accounts, per 100 people

Italy	Czech Republic	Portugal	Ukraine	UK
135.1	128.3	126.3	119.5	118.4

Country that Watches the Most TV

UNITED STATES

Each household in the United States watches an average of 38.0 hours of TV per week. That's the equivalent of almost 82 straight days, or 2.5 months per year! The average adult watches about 4 hours per day, and the average child watches more than 3 hours. Some 98 percent of American households own at least 1 television, and about 54 percent of children have a set in their bedrooms. In one year, a child will see about 30,000 commercials. By age 65, a person will have watched more than 2 million television ads.

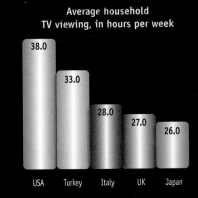

Countries that Watch the Most TV

Average household TV viewing, in hours per week

USA	Turkey	Italy	UK	Japan
38.0	33.0	28.0	27.0	26.0

World's Highest Television Ownership Rate

NORWAY

There is at least one television set in 99.97 percent of Norway's households. About 82 percent of Norwegians watch TV every day—almost four times the number of people who report reading a book. In total, each person watches about 18 hours of TV each week, averaging about 2.5 hours a day. There are approximately 360 television broadcast stations in the country and 2 million receivers. Only about 20 percent of Norway's population subscribes to cable television.

World's Highest Television Ownership Rates

Percentage of homes with television sets

Norway	Switzerland	Greece	Spain	Netherlands
99.97	99.83	99.50	99.48	99.42

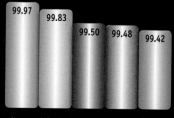

143

RECORDS

World's Largest Diamond

GOLDEN JUBILEE

The Golden Jubilee is the world's largest faceted diamond, with a weight of 545.67 carats. This gigantic gem got its name when it was presented to the king of Thailand in 1997 for the Golden Jubilee—or 50th anniversary celebration—of his reign. The diamond weighed 755.5 carats when it was discovered in a South African mine in 1986. Once it was cut, the diamond featured 148 perfectly symmetrical facets. The process took almost a year because of the diamond's size and multiple tension points. The diamond is on display at the Royal Museum of Bangkok in Thailand.

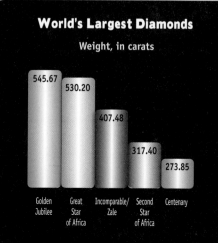

World's Largest Diamonds

Weight, in carats

Diamond	Weight
Golden Jubilee	545.67
Great Star of Africa	530.20
Incomparable/Zale	407.48
Second Star of Africa	317.40
Centenary	273.85

145

World's Tallest Mountain

MOUNT EVEREST

Mount Everest's tallest peak towers 29,035 feet (8,850 m) into the air, and it is the highest point on Earth. This peak is an unbelievable 5.5 miles (8.8 km) above sea level. Mount Everest is located in the Himalayas, on the border between Nepal and Tibet. The mountain got its official name from surveyor Sir George Everest. In 1953, Sir Edmund Hillary and Tenzing Norgay were the first people to reach the peak. In 2008, the Olympic torch was carried up to the top of the mountain on its way to the games in Beijing.

146

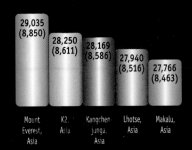

World's Tallest Mountains

Highest point, in feet (meters)

29,035 (8,850) — Mount Everest, Asia
28,250 (8,611) — K2, Asia
28,169 (8,586) — Kangchenjunga, Asia
27,940 (8,516) — Lhotse, Asia
27,766 (8,463) — Makalu, Asia

World's Tallest Volcano
OJOS DEL SALADO

Located on the border between Argentina and Chile, Ojos del Salado towers 22,595 feet (6,887 m) above the surrounding Atacama Desert. It is the second-highest peak in the Andean mountain chain. Ojos del Salado is a composite volcano, which means that it is a tall, symmetrical cone that was built by layers of lava flow, ash, and cinder. There is no record of the volcano erupting, but this could be because of the volcano's remote location. Ojos del Salado is a very popular spot for mountain climbing.

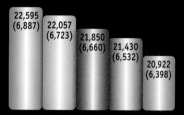

World's Tallest Volcanoes
Height, in feet (meters)

Ojos del Salado, Argentina/ Chile	Llullaillaco, Argentina/ Chile	Tipas, Argentina	Cerro el Cóndor, Argentina	Coropuna, Peru
22,595 (6,887)	22,057 (6,723)	21,850 (6,660)	21,430 (6,532)	20,922 (6,398)

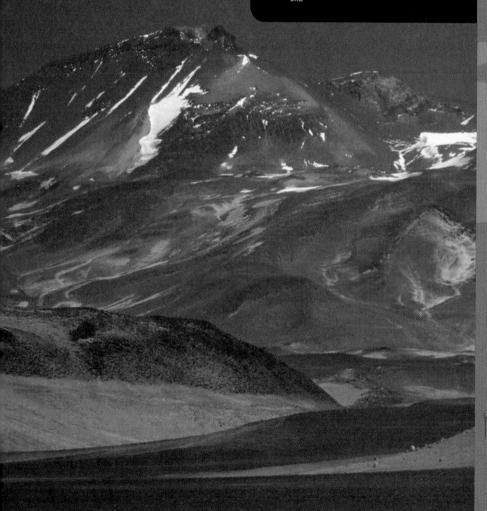

World's Largest Lake
CASPIAN SEA

This giant inland body of salt water stretches for almost 750 miles (1,207 km) from north to south, with an average width of about 200 miles (322 km). All together, it covers an area that's almost the same size as the state of California. The Caspian Sea is located east of the Caucasus Mountains in Central Asia. It is bordered by Iran, Russia, Kazakhstan, Azerbaijan, and Turkmenistan. The Caspian Sea has an average depth of about 550 feet (170 m). It is an important fishing resource, with species including sturgeon, salmon, perch, herring, and carp. Other animals living in the Caspian Sea include porpoises, seals, and tortoises. The sea is estimated to be 30 million years old and became landlocked 5.5 million years ago.

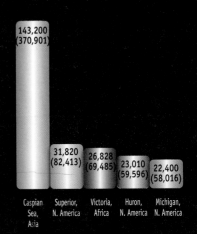

World's Largest Lakes

Approximate area, in square miles (square kilometers)

Lake	Area
Caspian Sea, Asia	143,200 (370,901)
Superior, N. America	31,820 (82,413)
Victoria, Africa	26,828 (69,485)
Huron, N. America	23,010 (59,596)
Michigan, N. America	22,400 (58,016)

World's Largest Desert

SAHARA

Located in northern Africa, the Sahara Desert covers approximately 3.5 million square miles (9.1 million sq km). It stretches for 5,200 miles (8,372 km) through the countries of Morocco, Algeria, Tunisia, Libya, Egypt, Mauritania, Mali, Niger, Chad, and Sudan. The Sahara gets very little rainfall—less than 8 inches (20 cm) per year. Even with its harsh environment, some 2.5 million people—mostly nomads—call the Sahara home. Date palms and acacias grow near oases. Some of the animals that live in the Sahara include gazelles, antelopes, jackals, foxes, and badgers.

World's Largest Deserts

Area, in millions of square miles (square kilometers)

Desert	Area
Sahara, Africa	3.5 (9.1)
Arabian, Asia	0.9 (2.3)
Gobi, Asia	0.5 (1.3)
Kalahari, Africa	0.36 (0.9)
Patagonia, South America	0.26 (0.67)

149

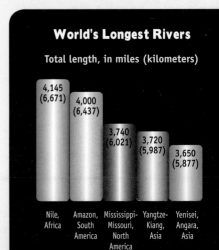

150

World's Longest River

NILE

The Nile River in Africa stretches 4,145 miles (6,671 km) from the tributaries of Lake Victoria in Tanzania and Uganda out to the Mediterranean Sea. Because of varying depths, boats can sail on only about 2,000 miles (3,217 km) of the river. The Nile flows through Rwanda, Uganda, Sudan, and Egypt. The river's water supply is crucial to the existence of these African countries. The Nile's precious water is used to irrigate crops and to generate electricity. The Aswan Dam and the Aswan High Dam—both located in Egypt—are used to store the autumn floodwater for later use. The Nile is also used to transport goods from city to city along the river.

World's Longest Rivers

Total length, in miles (kilometers)

Nile, Africa	Amazon, South America	Mississippi-Missouri, North America	Yangtze-Kiang, Asia	Yenisei, Angara, Asia
4,145 (6,671)	4,000 (6,437)	3,740 (6,021)	3,720 (5,987)	3,650 (5,877)

World's Largest Ocean
PACIFIC

The Pacific Ocean covers almost 64 million square miles (166 million sq km) and reaches 36,200 feet (11,000 m) below sea level at its greatest depth—the Mariana Trench (near the Philippines). In fact, this ocean is so large that it covers about one-third of the planet (more than all of Earth's land put together) and holds more than half of all the seawater on Earth. The United States could fit inside this ocean 18 times! Some of the major bodies of water included in the Pacific are the Bering Sea, the Coral Sea, the Philippine Sea, and the Gulf of Alaska.

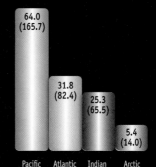

World's Largest Oceans

Approximate area, in millions of square miles (square kilometers)

64.0 (165.7)	31.8 (82.4)	25.3 (65.5)	5.4 (14.0)
Pacific Ocean	Atlantic Ocean	Indian Ocean	Arctic Ocean

World's Largest Island

GREENLAND

Located in the North Atlantic Ocean, Greenland covers more than 840,000 square miles (2,175,600 sq km). Not including continents, it is the largest island in the world. Its jagged coastline is approximately 24,400 miles (39,267 km) long—about the same distance as Earth's circumference at the equator. Mountain chains are located on Greenland's east and west coasts, and the coastline is indented by fjords, or thin bodies of water bordered by steep cliffs. From north to south, the island stretches for about 1,660 miles (2,670 km). About 700,000 square miles (1,813,000 sq km) of this massive island are covered by a giant ice sheet. The island also contains the world's largest national park—Northeast Greenland National Park—with an area of 375,291 square miles (972,000 sq km).

152

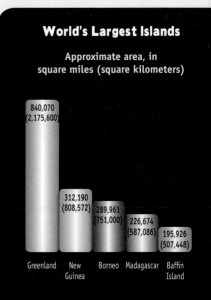

World's Largest Islands

Approximate area, in
square miles (square kilometers)

840,070
(2,175,600)

312,190
(808,572)

289,961
(751,000)

226,674
(587,086)

195,926
(507,448)

Greenland   New   Borneo Madagascar Baffin
Guinea   Island

Country with the Most Tropical Rain Forests

BRAZIL

Brazil—a large, tropical country in South America—has almost 1.16 million square miles (3.0 million sq km) of rain forest. The tropical forests of the Amazon River are located in the northern and north central areas of the country. Amazonia, the world's largest rain forest, spreads across half of Brazil. The rain forest is home to 2.5 million species of insect, 500 mammal species, 300 reptile species, and a third of the world's birds. The rain forest is threatened, however, by timber companies, the growing human population, and ranchers clearing land for their herds to graze.

Countries with the Most Tropical Rain Forests

Area of rain forest, in square miles (square kilometers)

Brazil, South America	Democratic Republic of Congo, Africa	Indonesia, Asia	Peru, South America	Bolivia, South America
1.16M (3.00M)	521,512 (1.35M)	343,029 (888,441)	292,032 (765,359)	265,012 (686,377)

153

World's Largest Crustacean

GIANT SPIDER CRAB

The giant spider crab has a 12-foot (3.7 m) leg span. That's almost wide enough to take up two parking spaces! The crab's body measures about 15 inches (38.1 cm) wide. Its ten long legs are jointed, and the first set has large claws at the end. The giant sea creature can weigh between 35 and 44 pounds (16 and 20 kg). It feeds on dead animals and shellfish it finds on the ocean floor. Giant spider crabs live in the deep water of the Pacific Ocean off southern Japan.

World's Largest Crustaceans
Leg span, in feet (meters)

12 (3.7)	5 (1.5)	4.5 (1.8)	3.0 (0.9)	2.5 (0.8)
Giant Spider Crab	Alaskan Red King Crab	Alaskan Blue King Crab	Alaskan Gold King Crab	Coconut Crab

World's Loudest Animal

BLUE WHALE

The loudest animal on Earth is the blue whale. The giant mammal's call can reach up to 188 decibels—about 40 decibels louder than a jet engine. The rumbling, low-frequency sounds of the blue whale can be heard for several hundred miles below the sea. Much of this whale chatter is used for communication, especially during the mating season. People cannot detect the whales' calls because they are too low-pitched for human ears.

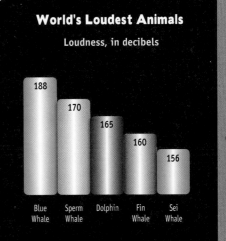

World's Loudest Animals

Loudness, in decibels

Blue Whale	Sperm Whale	Dolphin	Fin Whale	Sei Whale
188	170	165	160	156

World's Biggest Fish

WHALE SHARK

Although the average length of a whale shark is 30 feet (9 m), many have been known to reach up to 60 feet (18 m) long. That's the same length as two school buses! Whale sharks also weigh an average of 50,000 pounds (22,680 kg). As with most sharks, the females are larger than the males. Their mouths measure about 5 feet (1.5 m) long and contain about 3,000 teeth. Amazingly, these gigantic fish eat only microscopic plankton and tiny fish. They float near the surface looking for food.

World's Biggest Fish
Average weight, in pounds (kilograms)

Whale Shark	Basking Shark	Great White Shark	Greenland Shark	Tiger Shark
50,000 (22,680)	32,000 (14,515)	7,000 (3,175)	2,250 (1,020)	2,070 (939)

World's Most Dangerous Shark

GREAT WHITE

With a total of 237 unprovoked attacks on humans, great white sharks are the most dangerous predators in the sea. A great white can measure more than 20 feet (6.1 m) in length and weigh up to 3,800 pounds (1,723 kg). Because of the sharks' size, they can feed on large prey, including seals, dolphins, and even small whales. Often, when a human is attacked by a great white, it is because the shark has mistaken the person for its typical prey. The sharks make their homes in most waters throughout the world, but are most frequently found off the coasts of Australia, South Africa, California, and Mexico.

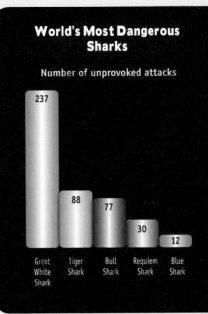

World's Most Dangerous Sharks

Number of unprovoked attacks

Great White Shark	Tiger Shark	Bull Shark	Requiem Shark	Blue Shark
237	88	77	30	12

Whale that Dives the Deepest

SPERM WHALE

Sperm whales can dive down to 10,500 feet (3,200 m) below the sea. The whales dive so deeply to hunt for giant squid to feed on. These dives last about 40 minutes, but a sperm whale can hold its breath for about an hour. The whales spend about 10 minutes at the surface of the water between deep dives. The sperm whale also holds the record for the largest animal brain, weighing in at about 20 pounds (9.1 kg). The whales can grow up to 60 feet (18.2 m) in length, and weigh up to 50 tons (45.4 t).

Whales that Dive the Deepest
Depth in feet (meters)

Sperm Whale	Beaked Whale	Beluga Whale	Humpback Whale	Bowhead Whale
10,500 (3,200)	6,500 (2,000)	2,100 (650)	700 (210)	500 (155)

World's Fastest Fish

SAILFISH

A sailfish once grabbed a fishing line and dragged it 300 feet (91 m) away in just three seconds. That means it was swimming at an average speed of 69 miles (109 km) per hour—higher than the average speed limit on a highway! Sailfish are very large—they average 6 feet (1.8 m) long, but can grow up to 11 feet (3.4 m). Sailfish eat squid and surface-dwelling fish. Sometimes several sailfish will work together to catch their prey. They are found in both the Atlantic and Pacific oceans and prefer a water temperature of about 80°F (27°C).

World's Fastest Fish

Maximum recorded speed, in miles (kilometers) per hour

Sailfish	Marlin	Mako Shark	Wahoo	Blue Shark
69 (109)	50 (80)	50 (80)	48 (78)	43 (69)

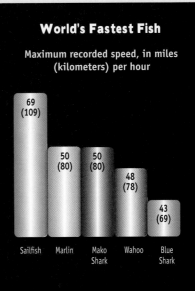

159

World's Fastest Shark
MAKO SHARK

A mako shark can cruise through the water at 50 miles (79.4 km) per hour. This super speed helps the shark catch its food, which consists mostly of tuna, herring, mackerel, swordfish, and porpoise. Occasionally makos even build up enough speed to leap out of the water. Mako sharks average 7 feet (2.1 m) in length, but can grow up to 12 feet (3.7 m) and weigh on average 1,000 pounds (454 kg). The sharks are found in temperate and tropical seas throughout the world.

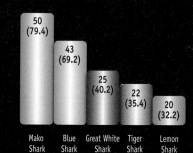

World's Fastest Sharks

Fastest speed, in miles (kilometers) per hour

Mako Shark	Blue Shark	Great White Shark	Tiger Shark	Lemon Shark
50 (79.4)	43 (69.2)	25 (40.2)	22 (35.4)	20 (32.2)

World's Heaviest Marine Mammal

BLUE WHALE

Blue whales are the largest animals that have ever inhabited Earth. They can weigh more than 143.3 tons (130 t) and measure over 100 feet (30 m) long. Amazingly, these gentle giants only eat krill—small, shrimplike animals. A blue whale can eat about 4 tons (3.6 t) of krill each day in the summer, when food is plentiful. To catch the krill, a whale gulps as much as 17,000 gallons (64,600 L) of seawater into its mouth at one time. Then it uses its tongue—which can be as big as a car—to push the water back out. The krill get caught in hairs on the whale's baleen (a keratin structure that hangs down from the roof of the whale's mouth).

World's Heaviest Marine Mammals

Weight, in tons (metric tons)

Blue Whale	Fin Whale	Right Whale	Sperm Whale	Gray Whale
143.3 (130)	49.6 (45)	44.1 (40)	39.7 (36)	36.0 (33)

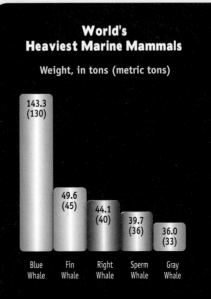

World's Largest Bird Wingspan
MARABOU STORK

With a wingspan that can reach up to 13 feet (4 m), the marabou stork has the largest wingspan of any bird. These large storks weigh up to 20 pounds (9 kg) and can grow up to 5 feet (150 cm) tall. Their long leg and toe bones are actually hollow. This adaptation is very important for flight because it makes the bird lighter. Although marabous eat insects, small mammals, and fish, the majority of their food is carrion—meat that is already dead. In fact, the stork's head and neck do not have any feathers. This helps the bird stay clean as it sticks its head into carcasses to pick out scraps of food.

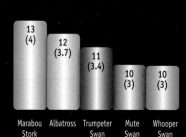

World's Largest Bird Wingspans

Wingspan, in feet (meters)

Marabou Stork	Albatross	Trumpeter Swan	Mute Swan	Whooper Swan
13 (4)	12 (3.7)	11 (3.4)	10 (3)	10 (3)

World's Fastest Flier

PEREGRINE FALCON

A peregrine falcon can reach speeds of up to 175 miles (282 km) per hour while diving through the air. That's about the same speed as the fastest race car in the Indianapolis 500. These powerful birds can catch prey in midair and kill it instantly with their sharp claws. Peregrine falcons range from about 13 to 19 inches (33 to 48 cm) long. The female is called a falcon, but the male is called a tercel, which means "one-third" in German. This is because the male is about one-third the size of the female.

World's Fastest Fliers

Top speed, in miles (kilometers) per hour

Peregrine Falcon	Spine-tailed Swift	Frigate Bird	Spur-winged Goose	Red-breasted Merganser
175 (282)	106 (171)	95 (153)	88 (142)	80 (129)

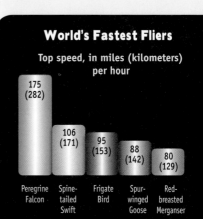

163

World's Longest Bird Migration
ARCTIC TERN

The arctic tern migrates from Maine to the coast of Africa, and then on to Antarctica, flying some 22,000 miles (35,406 km) a year. That's almost the same distance as the Earth's circumference. Some don't complete the journey, however—young terns fly the first half of the journey with their parents, but remain in Antarctica for a year or two. When they have matured, the birds fly back to Maine and the surrounding areas. Scientists are puzzled about how these birds remember the way back after only making the journey once, so early in their lives.

World's Longest Bird Migrations

Round-trip migration, in miles (kilometers)

Arctic Tern	White-rumped Sandpiper	Red Knot	Lesser Yellowleg	Swainson's Hawk
22,000 (35,406)	20,000 (32,187)	20,000 (32,187)	18,000 (28,968)	15,000 (24,140)

Bird that Builds the Largest Nest

BALD EAGLE

With a nest that can measure 8 feet (2.4 m) wide and 16 feet (4.9 m) deep, bald eagles have plenty of room to move around. These birds of prey have wingspans of up to 7.5 feet (2.3 m) and need a home that they can nest in comfortably. By carefully constructing their nest with sticks, branches, and plant material, a pair of bald eagles can balance their home—which can weigh up to 4,000 pounds (1,814 kg)—on the top of a tree or cliff. These nests are usually located by rivers or coastlines, the birds' watery hunting grounds. Called an aerie, this home will be used for the rest of the eagles' lives.

Birds that Build the Largest Nests

Nest diameter, in feet (meters)

Bald Eagle	Sociable Weaver	Maguari Stork	Great Blue Heron	Monk Parakeet
8 (2.4)	7 (2.1)	6 (1.8)	4.5 (1.4)	3 (0.9)

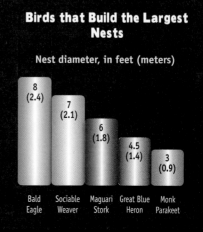

165

World's Largest Bird Egg
OSTRICH EGG

Ostriches—the world's largest birds—can lay eggs that measure 5 inches by 6 inches (13 cm by 16 cm) and weigh up to 4 pounds (1.8 kg). In fact, just one ostrich egg weighs as much as 24 chicken eggs. The egg yolk makes up one-third of the volume. Although the eggshell is only 0.08 inches (2 mm) thick, it is tough enough to withstand the weight of a 345-pound (157 kg) ostrich. A hen ostrich can lay from 10 to 70 eggs each year. Females are usually able to recognize their own eggs, even when they are mixed in with those of other females in their shared nest.

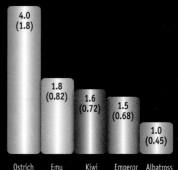

World's Largest Bird Eggs

Weight of egg, in pounds (kilograms)

Ostrich	Emu	Kiwi	Emperor Penguin	Albatross
4.0 (1.8)	1.8 (0.82)	1.6 (0.72)	1.5 (0.68)	1.0 (0.45)

World's Fastest Land Bird

OSTRICH

An ostrich can run at a top speed of 45 miles (72.4 km) per hour for about 30 minutes. This allows the speedy bird to easily outrun most predators. Its long, powerful legs help an ostrich cover 10 to 15 feet (3.1 to 4.6 km) per bound. And although it is a flightless bird, an ostrich uses its wings for balance when it runs. If an ostrich does need to defend itself, it has a kick powerful enough to kill a lion. The ostrich, which is also the world's largest bird at 10 feet (3.1 m) tall and 350 pounds (158.8 kg), is native to the savannas of Africa.

World's Fastest Land Birds

Speed, in miles (kilometers) per hour

Ostrich	Emu	Cassowary	Wild Turkey	Roadrunner
45 (72.4)	40 (64.4)	30 (48.2)	20 (32.2)	17 (27.4)

167

World's Heaviest Land Mammal

AFRICAN ELEPHANT

Weighing in at up to 14,430 pounds (6,545 kg) and measuring approximately 24 feet (7.3 m) long, African elephants are truly humongous. Even at their great size, they are strictly vegetarian. They will, however, eat up to 500 pounds (226 kg) of vegetation a day! Their two tusks—which are actually elongated teeth—grow continuously during their lives and can reach about 9 feet (2.7 m) in length. Elephants live in small groups of 8 to 15 family members with one female (called a cow) as the leader.

168

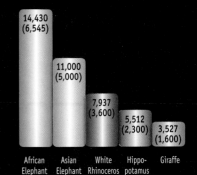

World's Heaviest Land Mammals

Weight, in pounds (kilograms)

African Elephant	Asian Elephant	White Rhinoceros	Hippo-potamus	Giraffe
14,430 (6,545)	11,000 (5,000)	7,937 (3,600)	5,512 (2,300)	3,527 (1,600)

World's Largest Rodent
CAPYBARA

Capybaras reach an average length of 4 feet (1.2 m), stand about 20 inches (51 cm) tall, and weigh between 75 and 150 pounds (34 to 68 kg)! That's about the same size as a Labrador retriever. Also known as water hogs and carpinchos, capybaras are found in South and Central America, where they spend much of their time in groups, looking for food. They are strictly vegetarian and have been known to raid gardens for melons and squash. Their partially webbed feet make capybaras excellent swimmers. They can dive down to the bottom of a lake or river to find plants and stay there for up to five minutes.

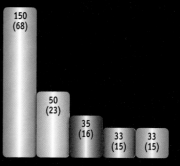

World's Largest Rodents

Weight, in pounds (kilograms)

Capybara	Beaver	Porcupine	Pacarana	Patagonian Cavy
150 (68)	50 (23)	35 (16)	33 (15)	33 (15)

World's Slowest Land Mammal

THREE-TOED SLOTH

A three-toed sloth can reach a top speed of only 0.07 miles (0.11 km) per hour while traveling on the ground. That means that it would take the animal almost 15 minutes to cross a four-lane street. The main reason sloths move so slowly is that they cannot walk like other mammals. They must pull themselves along the ground using only their sharp claws. Because of this, sloths spend the majority of their time in trees. There, they will sleep up to 18 hours each day. When they wake at night, they search for leaves and shoots to eat.

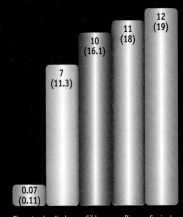

Some of the World's Slowest Land Mammals

Speed, in miles (kilometers) per hour

Three-toed Sloth	Koala	Gibbon	Pig	Squirrel
0.07 (0.11)	7 (11.3)	10 (16.1)	11 (18)	12 (19)

World's Fastest Land Mammal

CHEETAH

For short spurts, these sleek mammals can reach a speed of 65 miles (105 km) per hour. They can accelerate from 0 to 40 miles (64 km) per hour in just three strides. Their quickness easily enables these large African cats to outrun their prey. All other African cats must stalk their prey because they lack the cheetah's amazing speed. Unlike the paws of all other cats, cheetah paws do not have skin sheaths (thin protective coverings). Their claws, therefore, cannot be retracted.

World's Fastest Land Mammals

Speed, in miles (kilometers) per hour

Cheetah	Pronghorn Antelope	Mongolian Gazelle	Springbok	Grant's Gazelle/ Thompson's Gazelle
65 (105)	55 (89)	50 (80)	50 (80)	47 (76)

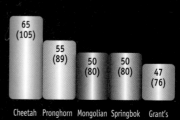

171

World's Tallest Land Animal
GIRAFFE

Giraffes are the giants among mammals, growing to more than 18 feet (5.5 m) in height. That means an average giraffe could look through the window of a two-story building. A giraffe's neck is 18 times longer than a human's, but both mammals have exactly the same number of neck bones. A giraffe's long legs enable it to outrun most of its enemies. When cornered, a giraffe has been known to kill a lion with a single kick to the head.

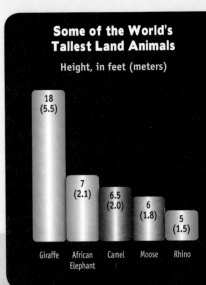

Some of the World's Tallest Land Animals
Height, in feet (meters)

Giraffe	African Elephant	Camel	Moose	Rhino
18 (5.5)	7 (2.1)	6.5 (2.0)	6 (1.8)	5 (1.5)

World's Largest Bat

GIANT FLYING FOX

The giant flying fox—a member of the megabat family—can have a wingspan of up to 6 feet (2 m). These furry mammals average just 7 wing beats per second, but can travel more than 40 miles (64 km) a night in search of food. Unlike smaller bats, which use echolocation, flying foxes rely on their acute vision and sense of smell to locate fruit, pollen, and nectar. Flying foxes got their name because their faces resemble a fox's face. Megabats live in the tropical areas of Africa, Asia, and Australia.

World's Largest Bats
Wingspan, in feet (meters)

Giant Flying Fox	Malayan Flying Fox	Golden Crown	Lyle's Flying Fox	Indian Flying Fox
6.0 (1.8)	5.7 (1.7)	5.5 (1.7)	5.0 (1.5)	4.4 (1.3)

173

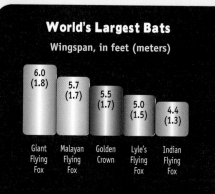

World's Deadliest Amphibian

POISON DART FROG

Poison dart frogs are found mostly in the tropical rain forests of Central and South America, where they live on the moist land. These lethal amphibians have enough poison to kill up to 20 humans. A dart frog's poison is so effective that native Central and South Americans sometimes coat their hunting arrows or hunting darts with it. These brightly colored frogs can be yellow, orange, red, green, blue, or any combination of these colors. They measure only 0.5 to 2 inches (1 to 5 cm) long. There are approximately 75 different species of poison dart frogs.

174

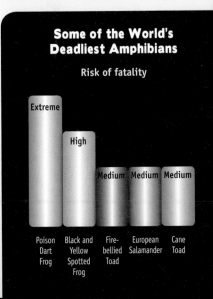

Some of the World's Deadliest Amphibians

Risk of fatality

Extreme	High	Medium	Medium	Medium
Poison Dart Frog	Black and Yellow Spotted Frog	Fire-bellied Toad	European Salamander	Cane Toad

World's Longest Snake
RETICULATED PYTHON

Some adult reticulated pythons can grow to 27 feet (8.2 m) long, but most reach an average length of 17 feet (5 m). That's almost the length of an average school bus! These pythons live mostly in Asia, from Myanmar to Indonesia to the Philippines. The python has teeth that curve backward and can hold the snake's prey still. It hunts mainly at night and will eat mammals and birds. Reticulated pythons are slow-moving creatures that kill their prey by constriction, or strangulation.

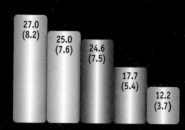

World's Longest Snakes
Maximum length, in feet (meters)

Reticulated Python	Anaconda	Rock Python	King Cobra	Oriental Rat Snake
27.0 (8.2)	25.0 (7.6)	24.6 (7.5)	17.7 (5.4)	12.2 (3.7)

Snake with the Longest Fangs

GABOON VIPER

The fangs of a Gaboon viper measure 2 inches (5 cm) in length! These giant fangs fold up against the snake's mouth so it does not pierce its own skin. When it is ready to strike its prey, the fangs snap down into position. The snake can grow up to 7 feet (2 m) long and weigh 18 pounds (8 kg). It is found in Africa and is perfectly camouflaged for hunting on the ground beneath leaves and grasses. The Gaboon viper's poison is not as toxic as some other snakes', but it is quite dangerous because of the amount of poison it can inject at one time. The snake is not very aggressive, however, and usually only attacks when bothered.

176

Snakes with the Longest Fangs

Fang length, in inches (centimeters)

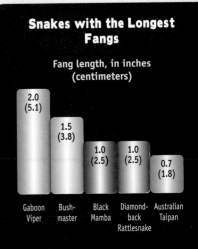

Gaboon Viper	Bush-master	Black Mamba	Diamond-back Rattlesnake	Australian Taipan
2.0 (5.1)	1.5 (3.8)	1.0 (2.5)	1.0 (2.5)	0.7 (1.8)

World's Deadliest Snake
BLACK MAMBA

With just one bite, an African black mamba snake releases a venom powerful enough to kill up to 200 humans. A bite from this snake is almost always fatal if it is not treated immediately. This large member of the cobra family grows to about 14 feet (4.3 m) long. In addition to its deadly poison, it is also a very aggressive snake. It will raise its body off the ground when it feels threatened. It then spreads its hood and strikes swiftly at its prey with its long front teeth. A black mamba is also very fast—it can move along at about 7 miles (11.7 km) per hour for short bursts.

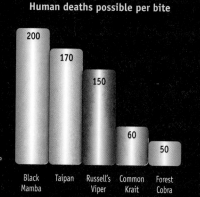

World's Deadliest Snakes

Human deaths possible per bite

Black Mamba	Taipan	Russell's Viper	Common Krait	Forest Cobra
200	170	150	60	50

World's Largest Amphibian
CHINESE GIANT SALAMANDER

With a length of 6 feet (1.8 m) and a weight of 55 pounds (25 kg), Chinese giant salamanders rule the amphibian world. This salamander has a large head, but its eyes and nostrils are small. It has short legs, a long tail, and very smooth skin. This large creature can be found in the streams of northeastern, central, and southern China. It feeds on fish, frogs, crabs, and snakes. The Chinese giant salamander will not hunt its prey. It will wait until a potential meal wanders too close and then grab it in its mouth. Because many people enjoy the taste of the salamander's meat, it is often hunted and its population is shrinking.

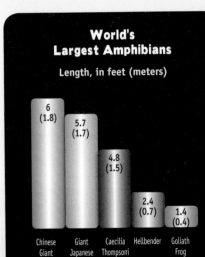

World's Largest Amphibians

Length, in feet (meters)

Chinese Giant Salamander	Giant Japanese Salamander	Caecilia Thompsoni	Hellbender	Goliath Frog
6 (1.8)	5.7 (1.7)	4.8 (1.5)	2.4 (0.7)	1.4 (0.4)

World's Longest-Lived Reptile

GALÁPAGOS TORTOISE

Some Galápagos tortoises have been known to live to the old age of 150 years. Galápagos tortoises are also some of the largest tortoises in the world, weighing in at up to 500 pounds (226 kg). These creatures are able to pull their heads, tails, and legs completely inside their shells. Amazingly, Galápagos tortoises can go without eating or drinking for many weeks. Approximately 10,000 of these tortoises live on the Galápagos island chain west of Ecuador.

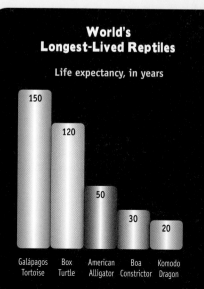

World's Longest-Lived Reptiles

Life expectancy, in years

Galápagos Tortoise	Box Turtle	American Alligator	Boa Constrictor	Komodo Dragon
150	120	50	30	20

179

World's Largest Lizard

KOMODO DRAGON

With a length of 10 feet (3 m) and a weight of 300 pounds (136 kg), Komodo dragons are the largest lizards roaming the Earth. A Komodo dragon has a long neck and tail, and strong legs. These members of the monitor family are found mainly on Komodo Island, located in the Lesser Sunda Islands of Indonesia. Komodos are dangerous and have even been known to attack and kill humans. A Komodo uses its sense of smell to locate food. It uses its long, yellow tongue to pick up an animal's scent. A Komodo can consume 80 percent of its body weight in just one meal!

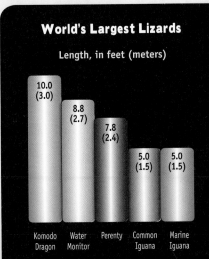

World's Largest Lizards

Length, in feet (meters)

10.0 (3.0)	8.8 (2.7)	7.8 (2.4)	5.0 (1.5)	5.0 (1.5)
Komodo Dragon	Water Monitor	Perenty	Common Iguana	Marine Iguana

World's Largest Reptile
SALTWATER CROCODILE

Saltwater crocodiles can grow to more than 22 feet (6.7 m) long. That's about twice the length of the average car. However, males usually measure only about 17 feet (5 m) long, and females normally reach about 10 feet (3 m) in length. A large adult will feed on buffalo, monkeys, cattle, wild boar, and other large mammals. Saltwater crocodiles are found throughout the East Indies and Australia. Despite their name, saltwater crocodiles can also be found in fresh water and swamps. Some other common names for this species are the estuary crocodile and the Indo-Pacific crocodile.

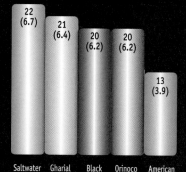

World's Largest Reptiles

Maximum length, in feet (meters)

Saltwater Crocodile	Gharial	Black Caiman	Orinoco Crocodile	American Alligator
22 (6.7)	21 (6.4)	20 (6.2)	20 (6.2)	13 (3.9)

World's Largest Spider
GOLIATH BIRDEATER

A Goliath birdeater is about the same size as a dinner plate—it can grow to a total length of 11 inches (28 cm) and weigh about 6 ounces (170 g). A Goliath's spiderlings are also big—they can have a 6-inch (15 cm) leg span after just one year. These giant tarantulas are found mostly in the rain forests of Guyana, Suriname, Brazil, and Venezuela. The Goliath birdeater's name is misleading—they commonly eat insects and small reptiles. Similar to other tarantula species, the Goliath birdeater lives in a burrow. The spider will wait by the opening to ambush prey that gets too close.

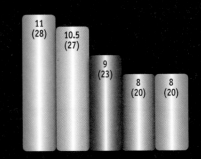

World's Largest Spiders

Length, in inches (centimeters)

Goliath Birdeater	Salmon Pink Birdeater	Slate Red Ornamental	King Baboon	Colombian Giant Redleg
11 (28)	10.5 (27)	9 (23)	8 (20)	8 (20)

World's Fastest-Flying Insect

HAWK MOTH

The average hawk moth—which got its name from its swift and steady flight—can cruise along at speeds over 33 miles (53 km) per hour. That's faster than the average speed limit on most city streets. Although they are found throughout the world, most species live in tropical climates. Also known as the sphinx moth and the hummingbird moth, this large insect can have a wingspan that reaches up to 8 inches (20 cm). The insect also has a good memory and may return to the same flowers at the same time each day.

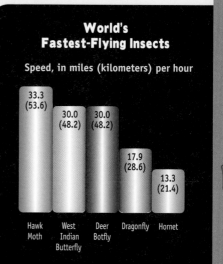

World's Fastest-Flying Insects

Speed, in miles (kilometers) per hour

Hawk Moth	West Indian Butterfly	Deer Botfly	Dragonfly	Hornet
33.3 (53.6)	30.0 (48.2)	30.0 (48.2)	17.9 (28.6)	13.3 (21.4)

183

World's Fastest-Running Insect
AUSTRALIAN TIGER BEETLE

Australian tiger beetles can zip along at about 5.7 miles (9.2 km) per hour—that's about 170 body lengths per second! If a human could run at the same pace, he or she would run about 340 miles (547.2 km) per hour. Australian tiger beetles use their terrific speed to run down prey. Once a meal has been caught, the beetle chews it up in its powerful jaws and coats it in digestive juice. When the prey has become soft, the tiger beetle rolls it together and eats it. These fierce beetles, which got their name from their skillful hunting, will also bite humans when provoked.

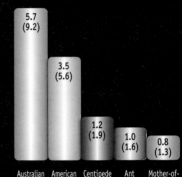

World's Fastest-Running Insects

Speed, in miles (kilometers) per hour

5.7 (9.2)	3.5 (5.6)	1.2 (1.9)	1.0 (1.6)	0.8 (1.3)
Australian Tiger Beetle	American Cockroach	Centipede	Ant	Mother-of-Pearl Caterpillar

World's Longest Insect Migration

MONARCH BUTTERFLY

Millions of monarch butterflies travel to Mexico from all parts of North America every fall, flying up to 2,700 miles (4,345 km). Once there, they will huddle together in the trees and wait out the cold weather. In spring and summer, most butterflies only live four or five weeks as adults, but in the fall, a special generation of monarchs is born. These butterflies will live for about seven months and participate in the great migration to Mexico. Scientists are studying these butterflies in the hope of learning how the insects know where and when to migrate to a place they have never visited before.

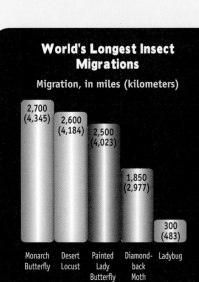

World's Longest Insect Migrations

Migration, in miles (kilometers)

Monarch Butterfly	Desert Locust	Painted Lady Butterfly	Diamond-back Moth	Ladybug
2,700 (4,345)	2,600 (4,184)	2,500 (4,023)	1,850 (2,977)	300 (483)

185

United States' Most Popular Dog Breed

LABRADOR RETRIEVER

There are 123,760 Labrador retrievers registered in the United States. That's almost the same amount as the next three most popular breeds added together. Labs are known for their companionship and good-natured personality, which is why many US families choose them for a pet. Labs are very intelligent, and often work as guide dogs for the blind, as well as on search-and-rescue teams. They are also excellent water dogs, and were originally used by fishermen to pull in their nets. The three types of labs are yellow, black, and chocolate, and each type can weigh up to 75 pounds (34 kg).

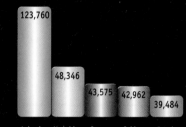

United States' Most Popular Dog Breeds

Number of registrations

Labrador Retriever	Yorkshire Terrier	German Shepherd	Golden Retriever	Beagle
123,760	48,346	43,575	42,962	39,484

United States' Most Popular Purebred Cat Breed

PERSIAN

Persians far outnumber all other types of registered purebred breeds, with 23,362 cats registered in the United States. These beautiful, long-haired cats were first kept as pets in Persia in the 1600s. They vary greatly in color, ranging from silver to brown. Persians have short legs, flat faces, and big, round eyes. They are known to have calm and friendly personalities, which makes them excellent family pets. However, because of their long hair, they need a lot of grooming.

United States' Most Popular Purebred Cat Breeds

Number of registrations

Breed	Number
Persian	23,362
Maine Coon	4,485
Exotic	2,321
Siamese	1,986
Abyssinian	1,609

United States' Greatest Annual Snowfall

MOUNT RAINIER

Mount Rainier had a record snowfall of 1,224 inches (3,109 cm) between February 1971 and February 1972. That's enough snow to cover a ten-story building! Located in the Cascade Mountains of Washington State, Mount Rainier is actually a volcano buried under 35 square miles (90.7 sq km) of snow and ice. The mountain, which covers about 100 square miles (259 sq km), reaches a height of 14,410 feet (4,392 m). Its three peaks include Liberty Cap, Point Success, and Columbia Crest. Mt. Rainier National Park was established in 1899.

United States' Greatest Annual Snowfalls

Highest annual snowfall, in inches (centimeters)

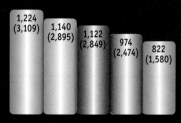

Mount Rainier, Washington, Feb. 1971–Feb. 1972	Mount Baker, Washington, 1998–1999	Paradise Station, Washington, July 1, 1971– June 30, 1972	Thompson Pass, Alaska, 1952–1953	Crater Lake National Park, Oregon 1948–1949
1,224 (3,109)	1,140 (2,895)	1,122 (2,849)	974 (2,474)	822 (1,580)

World's Coldest Inhabited Place

RESOLUTE

The residents of Resolute, Canada, have to bundle up—the average annual temperature is just -11.6°F (-24.2°C). Located on the northeast shore of Resolute Bay on the south coast of Cornwallis Island, the community is commonly the starting point for expeditions to the North Pole. In the winter it can stay dark for 24 hours, and in the summer it can stay light during the entire night. Only about 200 people brave the climate year-round, but the area is becoming quite popular with tourists.

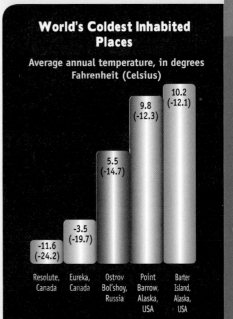

World's Coldest Inhabited Places

Average annual temperature, in degrees Fahrenheit (Celsius)

Resolute, Canada	Eureka, Canada	Ostrov Bol'shoy, Russia	Point Barrow, Alaska, USA	Barter Island, Alaska, USA
-11.6 (-24.2)	-3.5 (-19.7)	5.5 (-14.7)	9.8 (-12.3)	10.2 (-12.1)

189

World's Hottest Inhabited Place

DALLOL

Throughout the year, temperatures in Dallol, Ethiopia, in Africa average 93.2°F (34.0°C). Dallol is at the northernmost tip of the Great Rift Valley. The Dallol Depression reaches 328 feet (100 m) below sea level, making it the lowest point below sea level that is not covered by water. The area also has several active volcanoes. The only people to inhabit the region are the Afar, who have adapted to the harsh conditions there. For instance, to collect water the women build covered stone piles and wait for condensation to form on the rocks.

190

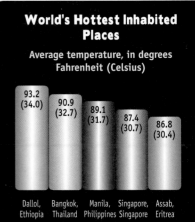

World's Hottest Inhabited Places

Average temperature, in degrees Fahrenheit (Celsius)

Dallol, Ethiopia	Bangkok, Thailand	Manila, Philippines	Singapore, Singapore	Assab, Eritrea
93.2 (34.0)	90.9 (32.7)	89.1 (31.7)	87.4 (30.7)	86.8 (30.4)

World's Wettest Inhabited Place
CHERRAPUNJI

Each year, some 498 inches (1,265 cm) of rain falls on Cherrapunji, India. That's enough rain to fill a four-story building! Most of the region's rain falls within a six-month period, during the monsoon season. It's not uncommon for constant rain to pelt the area for two months straight without even a ten-minute break. During the other six months, the winds change and carry the rain away from Cherrapunji, leaving the ground dry and dusty. Ironically, this causes a drought throughout most of the area.

World's Wettest Inhabited Places

Average annual rainfall, in inches (centimeters)

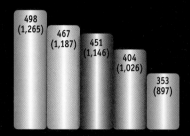

Cherrapunji, India	Mawsynram, India	Waialeale, Hawaii	Debundscha, Cameroon	Quibdo, Colombia
498 (1,265)	467 (1,187)	451 (1,146)	404 (1,026)	353 (897)

World's Driest Inhabited Place

ASWAN

Each year, only 0.02 inches (0.5 mm) of rain falls on Aswan, Egypt. In the country's sunniest and southernmost city, summer temperatures can reach a blistering 114°F (46°C). Aswan is located on the west bank of the Nile River, and it has a very busy marketplace that is also popular with tourists. The Aswan High Dam, at 12,565 feet (3,830 m) long, is the city's most famous landmark. It produces the majority of Egypt's power in the form of hydroelectricity.

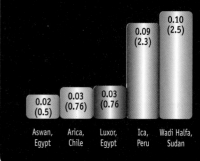

World's Driest Inhabited Places

Average annual rainfall, in inches (millimeters)

Aswan, Egypt	Arica, Chile	Luxor, Egypt	Ica, Peru	Wadi Halfa, Sudan
0.02 (0.5)	0.03 (0.76)	0.03 (0.76)	0.09 (2.3)	0.10 (2.5)

Place with the World's Fastest Winds

MOUNT WASHINGTON

The wind gusts at the top of Mount Washington reached 231 miles (372 km) per hour in 1934—and these gusts were not part of a storm. Normally, the average wind speed at the summit of this mountain is approximately 36 miles (58 km) per hour. Located in the White Mountains of New Hampshire, Mount Washington is the highest peak in New England at 6,288 feet (1,917 m). The treeless summit, which is known for its harsh weather, has an average annual temperature of only 26.5°F (-3.1°C).

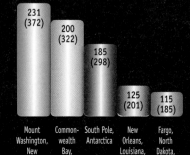

Places with the World's Fastest Winds

Speed of strongest winds, in miles (kilometers) per hour

Mount Washington, New Hampshire, USA	Common-wealth Bay, Antarctica	South Pole, Antarctica	New Orleans, Louisiana, USA	Fargo, North Dakota, USA
231 (372)	200 (322)	185 (298)	125 (201)	115 (185)

World's Tallest Cactus

SAGUARO

Many saguaro cacti grow to a height of 50 feet (15 m), but some have actually reached 75 feet (23 m). That's taller than a seven-story building. Saguaros start out quite small and grow very slowly. A saguaro only reaches about 1 inch (2.5 cm) high during its first 10 years. It will not bloom until it is between 50 and 75 years old. By this time, the cactus has a strong root system that can support about 9 to 10 tons (8 to 9 t) of growth. Its spines can measure up to 2.5 inches (5 cm) long. Saguaro cacti live for about 170 years. The giant cacti can be found from southeastern California to southern Arizona.

194

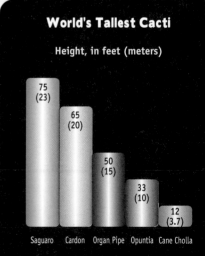

World's Tallest Cacti

Height, in feet (meters)

Saguaro	Cardon	Organ Pipe	Opuntia	Cane Cholla
75 (23)	65 (20)	50 (15)	33 (10)	12 (3.7)

World's Tallest Tree
CALIFORNIA REDWOOD

Growing in both California and southern Oregon, California redwoods can reach a height of 385 feet (117.4 m). Their trunks can grow up to 25 feet (7.6 m) in diameter. The tallest redwood on record is more than 60 feet (18.3 m) taller than the Statue of Liberty. Amazingly, this giant tree grows from a seed the size of a tomato. Some redwoods are believed to be more than 2,000 years old. The trees' thick bark and foliage protect them from natural hazards such as insects and fires.

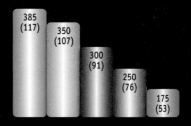

World's Tallest Tree Species

Height, in feet (meters)

California Redwood	Giant Sequoia	Eucalyptus	Douglas Fir	Japanese Cedar
385 (117)	350 (107)	300 (91)	250 (76)	175 (53)

World's Most Poisonous Mushroom

DEATH CAP

Death cap mushrooms are members of the Amanita family, which are among the most dangerous mushrooms in the world. The death cap contains deadly peptide toxins that cause rapid loss of bodily fluids and intense thirst. Within six hours, the poison shuts down the kidneys, liver, and central nervous system, causing coma and—in more than 50 percent of cases—death. Estimates of the number of poisonous mushroom species range from 80 to 2,000. Most experts agree, however, that at least 100 varieties will cause severe symptoms and even death if eaten.

196

World's Most Poisonous Mushrooms

Risk of fatality if consumed

Death Cap	Destroying Angel	Amanita Alba	Fly Agaric	Deadly Galerina
Extreme	Very High	High	Medium	Low

World's Largest Flower
RAFFLESIA

The blossoms of the giant rafflesia—or "stinking corpse lily"—can reach 36 inches (91 cm) in diameter and weigh up to 25 pounds (11 kg). Its petals can grow 1.5 feet (0.5 m) long and 1 inch (2.5 cm) thick. There are 16 different species of rafflesia. This endangered plant is found only in the rain forests of Borneo and Sumatra. It lives inside the bark of host vines and is noticeable only when its flowers break through to blossom. The large, reddish-purple flowers give off a smell similar to rotting meat, which attracts insects to help spread the rafflesia's pollen.

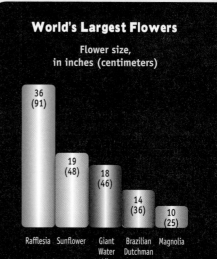

World's Largest Flowers

Flower size,
in inches (centimeters)

Flower	Size
Rafflesia	36 (91)
Sunflower	19 (48)
Giant Water Lily	18 (46)
Brazilian Dutchman	14 (36)
Magnolia	10 (25)

World's Deadliest Plant

CASTOR BEAN

The castor bean plant produces seeds that contain a protein called ricin. Scientists estimate that ricin is about 6,000 times more poisonous than cyanide and 12,000 times more poisonous than rattlesnake venom. It would take a particle of ricin only about the size of a grain of sand to kill a 160-pound (73 kg) adult. The deadly beans are actually quite pretty and are sometimes used in jewelry. Castor bean plants grow in warmer climates and can reach a height of about 10 feet (3 m). Their leaves can measure up to 2 feet (0.6 m) wide.

World's Deadliest Plants

Risk of fatality if consumed

Castor Bean	Rosary Bead	Foxglove	Azalea	English Ivy
Extreme	High	High	Medium	Low

World's Largest Seed
COCO DE MER

Measuring 3 feet (1 m) in diameter and 12 inches (30 cm) in length, the giant, dark brown seed of the coco de mer palm tree can weigh up to 40 pounds (18 kg). Only a few thousand seeds are produced each year. Coco de mer trees are found on the island of Praslin in the Seychelles Archipelago of the Indian Ocean. The area where some of the few remaining trees grow has been declared a Natural World Heritage Site in an effort to protect the species from poachers looking for the rare seeds. The tree can grow up to 100 feet (31 m) tall, with leaves measuring 20 feet (6 m) long and 12 feet (3.6 m) wide.

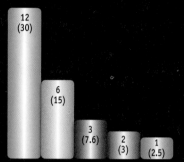

Some of the World's Largest Seeds

Length, in inches (centimeters)

Coco de Mer	Coconut	Avocado	Peach	Acorn
12 (30)	6 (15)	3 (7.6)	2 (3)	1 (2.5)

World's Highest Tsunami Wave Since 1900

LITUYA BAY

A 1,720-foot (524-m) tsunami wave crashed down in Lituya Bay, Alaska, on July 9, 1958. Located in Glacier Bay National Park, the tsunami was caused by a massive landslide that was triggered by an 8.3-magnitude earthquake. The water from the bay covered 5 square miles (13 sq km) of land and traveled inland as far as 3,600 feet (1,097 m). Millions of trees were washed away. Amazingly, because the area was very isolated and the coastline was sheltered by coves, only two people died when their fishing boat sank.

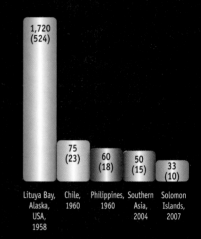

World's Highest Tsunami Waves Since 1900

Height of wave, in feet (meters)

Lituya Bay, Alaska, USA, 1958	Chile, 1960	Philippines, 1960	Southern Asia, 2004	Solomon Islands, 2007
1,720 (524)	75 (23)	60 (18)	50 (15)	33 (10)

World's Most Intense Earthquake Since 1900

COASTAL CHILE

An explosive earthquake measuring 9.5 on the Richter scale rocked the coast of Chile on May 22, 1960. This is equal to the intensity of about 60,000 hydrogen bombs. Some 2,000 people were killed and another 3,000 injured. The death toll was fairly low because the foreshocks frightened people into the streets. When the massive jolt came, many of the buildings that collapsed were already empty. The coastal towns of Valdivia and Puerto Montt suffered the most damage because they were closest to the epicenter—located about 100 miles (161 km) offshore.

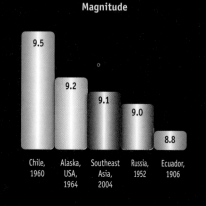

World's Most Intense Earthquakes Since 1900

Magnitude

Chile, 1960	Alaska, USA, 1964	Southeast Asia, 2004	Russia, 1952	Ecuador, 1906
9.5	9.2	9.1	9.0	8.8

201

World's Most Destructive Flood Since 1900

HURRICANE KATRINA

The pounding rain and storm surges of Hurricane Katrina resulted in catastrophic flooding that cost about $60 billion. The storm formed in late August 2005 over the Bahamas, moved across Florida, and finally hit Louisiana on August 29 as a category-three storm. The storm surge from the Gulf of Mexico flooded the state, as well as neighboring Alabama and Mississippi. Many levees could not hold back the massive amounts of water, and entire towns were destroyed. In total, some 1,800 people lost their lives.

202

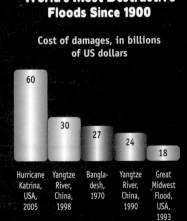

World's Most Destructive Floods Since 1900

Cost of damages, in billions of US dollars

60	30	27	24	18
Hurricane Katrina, USA, 2005	Yangtze River, China, 1998	Bangla-desh, 1970	Yangtze River, China, 1990	Great Midwest Flood, USA, 1993

World's Worst Oil Spill

AMOCO CADIZ

On March 16, 1978, the *Amoco Cadiz* hit ground in shallow water off the coast of Brittany, France, and spilled 220,000 tons (199,581 t) of oil into the English Channel. The very large crude carrier encountered strong storms and lost the ability to steer. Tugboats and the ship's anchor were unable to stop the tanker from drifting, and it collided with the rocky shore. The ship's hull and storage tanks were ripped open, and 68.7 million gallons (260 million L) of oil spread across 125 miles (201 km) of the Brittany coastline. The oil slick ruined fisheries, oyster beds, and surrounding beaches.

World's Worst Oil Spills

Oil spilled, in tons (metric tons)

Amoco Cadiz, Brittany, France 1978	Atlantic Empress, Tobago, 1979	Torrey Canyon, Isles of Scilly, UK, 1967	Braer, Shetland Isles UK, 1993	Sea Empress, Milford Haven, UK, 1996
220,000 (199,581)	160,000 (145,150)	119,000 (107,955)	85,000 (77,111)	72,000 (65,317)

World's Most Destructive Tornado Since 1900

OKLAHOMA CITY

On May 3, 1999, a devastating tornado swept through downtown Oklahoma City, Oklahoma, killing 36 people and causing more than $1.2 billion in damages. This powerful twister traveled almost 38 miles (61 km) in four hours and measured a mile (1.6 km) wide at times. With raging winds reaching 318 miles (512 km) per hour, it was the strongest wind speed ever recorded. More than 800 houses were destroyed in Oklahoma City alone. Because of the mass destruction caused by this twister, it was classified as a five—the second-highest possible rating—on the Fujita Tornado Scale.

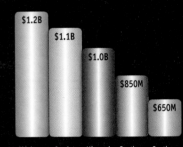

World's Most Destuctive Tornadoes Since 1900

Cost of damages, in US dollars

$1.2B	$1.1B	$1.0B	$850M	$650M
Oklahoma City, Oklahoma, 1999	Omaha, Nebraska, 1975	Missouri, Illinois, Indiana, 1925	Southern United States, 2008	Southern United States, 2006

Hurricane Camille

World's Most Intense Hurricanes Since 1900

HURRICANE ALLEN & HURRICANE CAMILLE

Both Hurricane Allen and Hurricane Camille were category-five storms with winds that gusted up to 190 miles (306 km) per hour. Hurricane Camille made landfall in the United States along the mouth of the Mississippi River on August 17, 1969. Mississippi and Virginia sustained the most damage, and the total storm damages cost $1.42 billion. Hurricane Allen sustained its strongest winds near Puerto Rico on August 5, 1980. The storm traveled through the Caribbean, Cuba, the Yucatan Peninsula, and the south-central United States. The damages totaled about $1 billion.

World's Most Intense Hurricanes Since 1900

Highest sustained wind speed, in miles (kilometers) per hour

Hurricane Allen, 1980	Hurricane Camille, 1969	Hurricane Gilbert, 1988	Hurricane Mitch, 1998	Hurricane Katrina, 2005
190 (306)	190 (306)	184 (296)	180 (290)	175 (282)

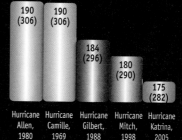

Country that Consumes the Most Energy Drinks

JAPAN

In Japan, each person consumes an average of 3.9 gallons (14.8 L) of energy drinks each year. This totals more than 499 million gallons (1,889 L) for everyone in the country. Energy drinks have been popular in Japan for several decades, and they are consumed as frequently as soda or fruit juice. They are also less expensive there than they are in the United States. About 60 percent of all energy drinks are sold from vending machines, and the most popular flavors are Coca-Cola's Real Gold, Otsuka's Oranamin C, and Suntory's Deka Vita C.

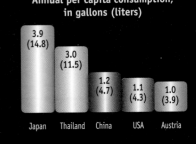

Countries that Consume the Most Energy Drinks

Annual per capita consumption, in gallons (liters)

Japan	Thailand	China	USA	Austria
3.9 (14.8)	3.0 (11.5)	1.2 (4.7)	1.1 (4.3)	1.0 (3.9)

Country that Drinks the Most Bottled Water

UNITED ARAB EMIRATES

The people in the United Arab Emirates, or UAE, each drink an average of 68.6 gallons (260 l) of bottled water each year. With a population of about 4.6 million people, that totals about 315.5 million gallons (1.2 billion l) for the country annually. Residents can get very thirsty in the UAE's hot and dry climate, with summer temperatures sometimes reaching 118° F (48° C). The UAE also has a healthy economy and many popular tourist spots, creating a strong market for bottled water. Worldwide bottled water sales are down on a whole, however, since more people view the containers as an environmental threat.

Countries that Drink the Most Bottled Water

Annual per capita consumption, in gallons (liters)

United Arab Emirates	Mexico	Italy	Belgium	France
68.6 (259.7)	54.1 (204.8)	40.9 (155.0)	39.5 (149.5)	35.8 (135.5)

Country that Consumes the Most Soft Drinks

UNITED STATES

Americans have an annual per capita soft drink consumption of 40.9 gallons (155.0 L). This means that each person in the country drinks an average of 436 cans of soda each year. Soda accounts for about 25 percent of all drinks consumed in the United States. About 75 percent of all soda is sold in containers, and the rest is sold through drink fountains. Recent studies show that diet sodas, as well as flavored sodas such as cherry, orange, and root beer, are becoming more popular than colas. The country's three top-selling soft drink companies are the Coca-Cola Company, PepsiCo Inc., and Dr Pepper/7UP.

Countries that Consume the Most Soft Drinks

Annual per capita consumption, in gallons (liters)

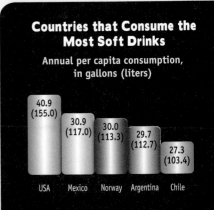

USA	Mexico	Norway	Argentina	Chile
40.9 (155.0)	30.9 (117.0)	30.0 (113.3)	29.7 (112.7)	27.3 (103.4)

Country that Eats the Most Chocolate

UNITED KINGDOM

Each person in the United Kingdom eats about 22.8 pounds (10.3 kg) of chocolate annually. The UK enjoys a combined total of 1.38 billion pounds (63 million kg) each year, which accounts for about 30 percent of all the chocolate eaten in all Europe. Bar chocolate, such as Snickers and a local Crunchie brand, account for about 45 percent of all sales. Dark chocolate sales have also increased recently due to reports that it is healthier than milk and white chocolate. One of the main contributors to the UK chocolate market is the Cadbury company, which uses more than 112 million pounds (51 million kg) of cocoa beans each year.

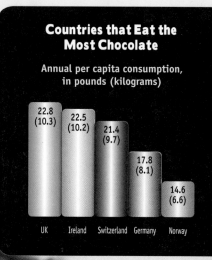

Countries that Eat the Most Chocolate

Annual per capita consumption, in pounds (kilograms)

UK	Ireland	Switzerland	Germany	Norway
22.8 (10.3)	22.5 (10.2)	21.4 (9.7)	17.8 (8.1)	14.6 (6.6)

Country that Eats the Most Ice Cream

NEW ZEALAND

The per capita consumption of ice cream in New Zealand is 59.2 pints (28 l) each year. That's more than a pint a week! New Zealand also makes a lot of ice cream—about tons per year. The top flavors in New Zealand include vanilla, hokey pokey (vanilla with toffee bits), chocolate, and strawberry. Frozen treats were first served in the Roman Empire when people mixed fruit with ice. In the eighteenth century, ice cream became popular in France, England, and the United States. The ice cream cone was first served in 1904 at the World's Fair in St. Louis, Missouri. Today, frozen dessert sales total billions of dollars worldwide.

Countries that Eat the Most Ice Cream

Annual per capita consumption, in pints (liters)

New Zealand	USA	Scandinavia	Germany	Greece
59.2 (28)	52.8 (25)	35.9 (17)	16.9 (8)	9.5 (4.5)

Country that Eats the Most Meat

SPAIN

The people of Spain like their meat—each person in the country eats about 251 pounds (113.8 kg) annually. This means that the country consumes a total of 10.1 billion pounds (4.5 billion kg) of beef, chicken, pork, and other meat each year—about the same weight as 6.8 million cows. Central Spain enjoys the most meat, including roasted lamb, goat, and pig. Stews, paella, jamón serrano (cured ham), and chorizo (seasoned sausage) are other popular ways that the people of Spain enjoy their meat.

Countries that Eat the Most Meat

Annual per capita consumption, in pounds (kilograms)

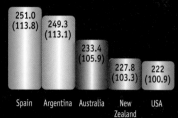

Spain	Argentina	Australia	New Zealand	USA
251.0 (113.8)	249.3 (113.1)	233.4 (105.9)	227.8 (103.3)	222 (100.9)

Country that Eats the Most Bread

TURKEY

The people of Turkey eat a lot of bread, averaging more than 320 pounds (145.1 kg) per capita each year. This means that the entire country goes through about 23 billion pounds (10.4 billion kg) of the starchy carbohydrate annually. Bread is eaten with every meal, and is served in several different ways. Turks often use bread to soak up their soup, and they also bake bread with fillings such as meat, cheese, or vegetables. Some of the most common breads include *pide* (similar to a pita), and a thin flat bread called *lavas*.

Countries that Eat the Most Bread

Annual per capita consumption, in pounds (kilograms)

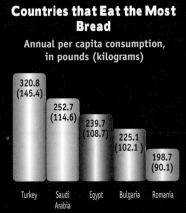

Turkey	Saudi Arabia	Egypt	Bulgaria	Romania
320.8 (145.4)	252.7 (114.6)	239.7 (108.7)	225.1 (102.1)	198.7 (90.1)

Country that Recycles the Most Paper
UNITED STATES

Each year the United States recycles about 49.2 million tons (44.6 million t) of paper—or 53 percent of all paper products produced. About 89 percent of all newspapers and 72 percent of corrugated cardboard are recycled in the country. Most of this is turned back into paper products, including newspapers, egg cartons, packing material, and insulation. The United States recycles paper to reduce landfill waste, reduce the number of trees that are cut down for paper production, and reduce pollution. There are more than 8,750 curbside recycling programs throughout the country.

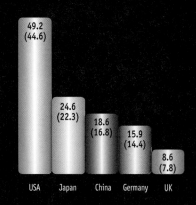

Countries that Recycle the Most Paper

Paper recycled annually, in millions of tons (metric tons)

USA	Japan	China	Germany	UK
49.2 (44.6)	24.6 (22.3)	18.6 (16.8)	15.9 (14.4)	8.6 (7.8)

MONEY
RECORDS

Most Expensive/Valuable
Bestsellers
Companies & Consumption

World's Most Expensive Restaurant

MASA

At this elegant Japanese restaurant, diners will enjoy a meal with an average cost of $400. Located in Manhattan's Time Warner Building, Masa has just 26 seats. There are no menus here because the sushi chef—Masayoshi Takayama—prepares only what specialties are in season. Diners start with 5 appetizers, followed by a sushi entrée with at least 15 different types of seafood flown in from Japan. Masa opened in 2004 and serves lunch and dinner. If restaurant-goers would like to save a little money, Bar Masa is located next door and offers much more economical meals.

World's Most Expensive Restaurants

Average cost of a meal, in US dollars

Masa, New York City, USA	L'Arpege, Paris, France	Aragawa, Tokyo, Japan	Joel Rubuchon at the Mansion, Las Vegas, USA	El Bulli, Roses, Spain
400	395	375	360	270

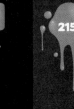

215

World's Most Valuable Baseball

MARK MCGWIRE'S 70TH HOME-RUN BASEBALL

Mark McGwire's 70th home-run baseball fetched $3.05 million at auction in January 1999. The bid, which was actually $2.7 million plus a large commission fee, is the most money paid for a sports artifact. The ball was only expected to sell for about $1 million. Businessman and baseball fan Todd McFarlane said he bought the ball because he wanted to own a piece of history. This famous baseball marked the end of the exciting 1998 home-run race between Mark McGwire and Sammy Sosa. Both beat Roger Maris's three-decade record of 61—Sosa with 66 and McGwire with 70.

World's Most Valuable Baseballs

Price paid at auction, in US dollars

Bar	Value
Mark McGwire's 70th of Season	3.05M
Babe Ruth's 1933 1st All-Star Game Home Run	805,000
Barry Bonds's 756th	752,467
Hank Aaron's 755th	650,000
Barry Bonds's 73rd of Season	517,500

World's Most Valuable Production Car

BUGATTI VEYRON 16.4

The Bugatti Veyron has a price tag of $1.2 million. That's just slightly less than buying a private jet! The Veyron is also one of the world's fastest cars. With a top speed of 253 miles (407.2 km) per hour, the Veyron can accelerate from 0 to 124 miles (200 km) per hour in just 7.3 seconds. Bugatti plans to make only 300 models of the Veyron. Despite the state of the global economy and the seven-figure price tag, the cars are selling quickly.

World's Most Valuable Production Cars

Base price, in US dollars

1.2M	667,00	654,000	645,000	555,000
Bugatti Veyron 16.4	Pagani Zonda C12F	SSC Ultimate Aero	Le Blanc Mirabeau	Saleen S7

217

218

World's Most Valuable Brand
COCA-COLA

Coca-Cola is worth more money than any other brand in the world, with a company value of nearly $67 billion. Coca-Cola is the largest nonalcoholic beverage company in the world, employing about 92,400 people. Besides soda, the company also produces water, juice, coffee, tea, and sports drinks. In fact, the company has more than 3,000 beverage products. They are ranked first in soda and juice sales, and second in sports-drink sales. Coca-Cola products are sold in nearly every country.

World's Most Valuable Brands

Brand value, in billions of US dollars

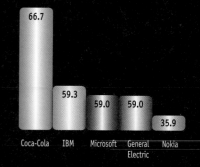

Coca-Cola	IBM	Microsoft	General Electric	Nokia
66.7	59.3	59.0	59.0	35.9

World's Bestselling eBay Item
NINTENDO WII

Bidders signed on to eBay in droves during 2008 to bid on the 2.05 million Nintendo Wii game consoles that were up for auction that year. The Wii was one of the hottest-selling items during the holiday season, and many people turned to the online auction site when stores sold out. On average, there are about 19 million items for sale on eBay at any given time. Some $729 worth of goods are sold every second. There are about 215 million eBay users worldwide, and more than half of them live in the United States.

World's Bestselling eBay Items

Number of items sold

2.05M	1.29M	281,361	223,139	212,837
Nintendo Wii	Xbox 360	Apple iPod Touch	Hannah Montana items	Apple iPhone 3G

World's Top-Selling Car Ever
TOYOTA COROLLA

The Toyota Corolla is the world's best-selling car in history, with more than 32 million vehicles sold. The Corolla was first produced in Japan in 1966; it was introduced in the United States in 1968, where it sold for about $1,700. During the car's 43-year history, Toyota has sold one Corolla about every 40 seconds somewhere in the world. Over the years, the car has been redesigned many times, most recently to make it larger and more appealing to younger buyers. Corollas are sold in approximately 160 countries.

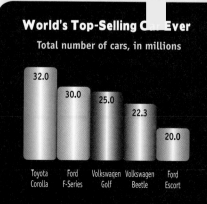

World's Top-Selling Car Ever
Total number of cars, in millions

Toyota Corolla	Ford F-Series	Volkswagen Golf	Volkswagen Beetle	Ford Escort
32.0	30.0	25.0	22.3	20.0

World's Most Profitable Company
EXXONMOBIL

Gasoline giant ExxonMobil made a ton of cash in 2008, raking in more than $40.6 billion. The company recorded some $372 billion in sales. ExxonMobil produces, transports, and sells crude oil and natural gas worldwide. It also manufactures and sells petroleum products across the globe. In addition, Mobil 1 is the world's most successful motor oil. ExxonMobil has 40 oil refineries in 20 countries and is capable of producing 6.4 million barrels of oil each day. They provide fuel to about 35,000 service stations, some 700 airports, and more than 200 ports.

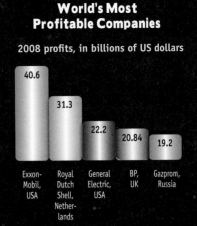

World's Most Profitable Companies

2008 profits, in billions of US dollars

40.6	Exxon-Mobil, USA
31.3	Royal Dutch Shell, Netherlands
22.2	General Electric, USA
20.84	BP, UK
19.2	Gazprom, Russia

Exxon Regular
Unleaded
$
Price per gallon
All taxes included
MINIMUM OCTANE RATING
(R+M)/2 METHOD
87
PRESS

Exxon Plus
Unleaded
$
Price per gallon
All taxes included
MINIMUM OCTANE RATING
(R+M)/2 METHOD
89
PRESS

Exxon Supreme
Unleaded
$
Price per gallon
All taxes included
MINIMUM OCTANE RATING
(R+M)/2 METHOD
91
PRESS

WARNING

Country that Spends the Most on Toys

UNITED STATES

The toy industry is booming in the United States. In 2008, Americans spent an amazing $21.6 billion on toys! That's equivalent to every single person in the country buying $72 worth of toys. It's not too much of a surprise considering toys are sold practically everywhere, from grocery stores to hardware stores. November and December account for about 40 percent of the total toy sales for the year. The United States accounts for 33 percent of worldwide toy sales, followed by Europe with 27 percent of sales.

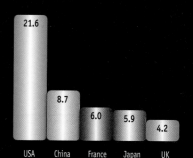

Countries that Spend the Most on Toys

Total spending, in billions of US dollars

USA	China	France	Japan	UK
21.6	8.7	6.0	5.9	4.2

Largest International Food Franchise
MCDONALD'S

There are more than 31,377 McDonald's restaurants in the world, serving customers in 119 different countries. The company adds approximately 100 new franchises each year. About 70 percent of the restaurant franchises are run by local businesspeople. McDonald's serves about 52 million customers each day, about 23 million of whom are in the United States. Out of respect for local cultures, restaurants in different countries modify their menus according to religious or cultural traditions. For example, there is a kosher McDonald's in Jerusalem, and the Big Macs in India are made with lamb instead of beef.

Largest International Food Franchises

Number of franchises

McDonald's	Subway	Starbucks	KFC	Burger King
31,377	30,789	15,000	13,639	11,395

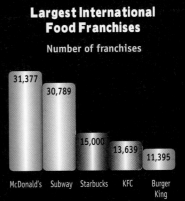

223

HUMAN-MADE RECORDS

Constructions
Travel
Transportation

Amusement Park with the Most Rides

CEDAR POINT

Located in Sandusky, Ohio, Cedar Point offers park visitors 74 rides to enjoy. Skyhawk—the park's newest ride—thrusts riders 125 feet (38 m) into the air and is the largest swing ride in the world. Top Thrill Dragster roller coaster is the tallest in the world at 420 feet (128 m). And with 17 roller coasters, Cedar Point also has the most coasters of any theme park in the world. Over 53,963 feet (16,448 m) of coaster track—more than 10 miles (16.1 km)—run through the park. In 2008, Cedar Point was named "Best Amusement Park in the World" by *Amusement Today* for the eleventh time.

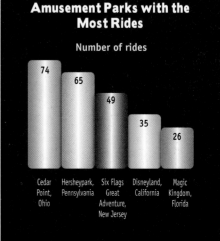

Amusement Parks with the Most Rides

Number of rides

Cedar Point, Ohio	Hersheypark, Pennsylvania	Six Flags Great Adventure, New Jersey	Disneyland, California	Magic Kingdom, Florida
74	65	49	35	26

225

City with the Most Skyscrapers

HONG KONG

A total of 199 skyscrapers rise high above the streets of Hong Kong. In fact, the world's fifth-tallest building—Two International Finance Centre—towers 1,362 feet (415 m) above the city. Because this bustling Chinese business center has only about 160 square miles (414 sq km) of land suitable for building, architects have to build up instead of out. And Hong Kong keeps growing—60 of the city's giant buildings were constructed in the last seven years. Some large development projects, such as the Sky Tower Apartment Complex, added seven skyscrapers to the landscape in just one year.

Cities with the Most Skyscrapers

Number of skyscrapers

City	Number
Hong Kong, China	199
New York City, New York, USA	190
Chicago, Illinois, USA	90
Shanghai, China	70
Tokyo, Japan	69

World's Tallest Apartment Building

Q1

Q1, a luxury apartment complex on Australia's Gold Coast, rises 1,058 feet (323 m) above the surrounding sand. There are 526 apartments within the building's 80 floors. Some apartments have glass-enclosed balconies. Q1 residents can enjoy Australia's only beachside observation deck and a 10-story sky garden. Some other amenities include retail outlets, a lagoon swimming pool, a spa, a sauna, and a fitness center. And just in case all nine elevators are out of order, there are 1,430 steps from the penthouse to the basement.

World's Tallest Apartment Buildings

Height, in feet (meters)

Building	Height
Q1, Gold Coast, Australia	1,058 (323)
Eureka Tower, Melbourne, Australia	975 (297)
21st Century Tower, UAE	883 (269)
Tower Palace Three, Tower G, Seoul, South Korea	866 (264)
Trump World Tower, New York City, USA	863 (263)

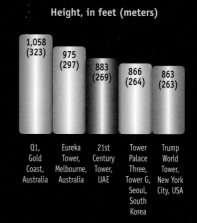

227

World's Largest Dome

02

Located in London, UK, the O2 has a roof that measures 1,050 feet (320 m) in diameter and covers 861,113 square feet (80,000 sq m). That's large enough to contain the Great Pyramid of Giza! The roof is made of 107,639 square feet (10,000 sq m) of fabric and is held up by 43 miles of steel cable. It also boasts a movie complex, theaters, and restaurants. The dome was built for the country's millennium celebration. After the New Year's celebration, renovations began to turn the dome into a sports complex, and it will be used for the 2012 Olympics.

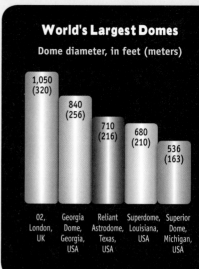

World's Largest Domes

Dome diameter, in feet (meters)

1,050 (320)	840 (256)	710 (216)	680 (210)	536 (163)
O2, London, UK	Georgia Dome, Georgia, USA	Reliant Astrodome, Texas, USA	Superdome, Louisiana, USA	Superior Dome, Michigan, USA

World's Tallest Habitable Building

BURJ DUBAI

The newly constructed Burj Dubai in the United Arab Emirates towers 2,684 feet (818 m) above the ground. With 110 floors, the building cost about $4.1 billion to construct. Both a hotel and apartments are housed inside the luxury building, which covers 500 acres (202 ha). The building will feature the world's fastest elevators, traveling at a speed of 40 miles (64 km) an hour. The tower supplies its occupants with about 250,000 gallons (66,043 L) of water a day, and will deliver enough electricity to power 360,000 100-watt light bulbs.

World's Tallest Habitable Buildings

Height, in feet (meters)

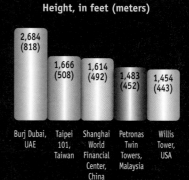

Burj Dubai, UAE	Taipei 101, Taiwan	Shanghai World Financial Center, China	Petronas Twin Towers, Malaysia	Willis Tower, USA
2,684 (818)	1,666 (508)	1,614 (492)	1,483 (452)	1,454 (443)

World's Largest Mall
SOUTH CHINA MALL

The South China Mall in Dongguan City covers 7.1 million square feet (0.66 million sq m) of retail and entertainment space. The megamall—which opened in 2005—was designed with seven major areas that resemble Amsterdam, Paris, Rome, Venice, Egypt, the Caribbean, and California. And, for shoppers too tired to walk from one end of the giant retail outlet to the other, there are gondolas and water taxis located on the mile-long, human-made canal that circles the perimeter. However, the mall, which was designed to showcase 1,500 stores, only houses about 20. Retailers have been slow to set up shop at the mall.

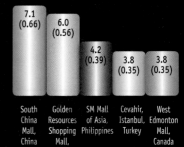

World's Largest Malls

Area, in millions of square feet (square meters)

South China Mall, China	Golden Resources Shopping Mall, China	SM Mall of Asia, Philippines	Cevahir, Istanbul, Turkey	West Edmonton Mall, Canada
7.1 (0.66)	6.0 (0.56)	4.2 (0.39)	3.8 (0.35)	3.8 (0.35)

World's Largest Library

LIBRARY OF CONGRESS

The Library of Congress is the largest library in the world, with more than 138 million items on approximately 650 miles (1046 km) of bookshelves. That means that the shelves could stretch from their home in Washington, DC, all the way to Chicago, Illinois! The collections include more than 32 million books and other print materials, 2.9 million recordings, 12.5 million photographs, 5.3 million maps, 5.5 million pieces of sheet music, and 61 million manuscripts. The Library receives about 22,000 items each business day, and adds approximately 10,000 items to the collections daily.

World's Largest Libraries

Number of books housed, in millions

Library of Congress, USA	British Library, England	Deutsche National-bibliothek, Germany	Library of the Russian Academy of Sciences, Russia	National Library of Canada, Canada
32.1	29.0	22.2	20.5	19.5

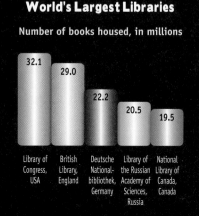

231

World's Largest Sports Stadium

RUNGRADO MAY FIRST STADIUM

The Rungrado May First Stadium, also known as the May Day Stadium, can seat up to 150,000 people. The interior of the stadium covers 2.2 million square feet (204,386 sq m). Located in Pyongyang, North Korea, this venue is mostly used for soccer matches and other athletic contests. It is named after Rungra Island, on which the stadium is located, in the middle of the Taedong River. When it is not being used for sporting events, the stadium is used for choreographed gymnastics known as Arirang.

232

World's Largest Sports Stadiums

Number of seats

Rungrado May First Stadium, North Korea	Salt Lake Stadium, India	Beaver Stadium, USA	Michigan Stadium, USA	Estadio Azteca, Mexico
150,000	120,000	107,282	106,201	105,000

World's Largest Restaurant
DAMASCUS GATE

With its 6,014 seats, Damascus Gate in Syria is by far the world's largest restaurant. During the busy summer months, the restaurant employs about 1,800 people to staff the 581,250 square-foot (54,000 sq m) dining area and 26,900 square-foot (2,500 sq m) kitchen. The open-air area features both waterfalls and fountains. The kitchen functions like a production line, and a single chef can prepare 25 to 30 servings of popular dishes—such as hummus—in about a minute. That's about one bowl every two seconds!

World's Largest Restaurants

Number of seats

Damascus Gate, Syria	The Royal Dragon Restaurant, Thailand	Das Dutchman Essenhaus, USA	Macau De Café, Philippines	Café de Macao, China
6,014	5,000	1,100	1,050	1,000

World's Largest Movie Theater
RADIO CITY MUSIC HALL

New York City's Radio City Music Hall is the largest single-screen theater in the world, with 5,933 seats. It's no wonder that the theater has become a hot spot for films. Since 1933, more than 700 movies have opened there, including *Mary Poppins*, *101 Dalmatians*, and *The Lion King*. The massive theater has a marquee that measures a full city block in length, and its auditorium is 160 feet (49 m) long. Its ceilings tower 84 feet (26 m) high. Since it first opened, more than 300 million people have attended shows and films there.

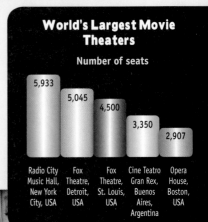

World's Largest Movie Theaters

Number of seats

5,933	5,045	4,500	3,350	2,907
Radio City Music Hall, New York City, USA	Fox Theatre, Detroit, USA	Fox Theatre, St. Louis, USA	Cine Teatro Gran Rex, Buenos Aires, Argentina	Opera House, Boston, USA

World's Top Tourist Country

FRANCE

France hosts almost 82 million tourists annually. That's about two and a half times the entire population of Canada! The most popular French destinations are Paris and the Mediterranean coast. In July and August—the most popular months to visit France—tourists flock to the westernmost coastal areas of the region. In the winter, visitors hit the slopes at major ski resorts in the northern Alps. Tourists also visit many of France's world-renowned landmarks and monuments, including the Eiffel Tower, Notre Dame, the Louvre, and the Palace of Versailles. Most tourists are from other European countries, especially Germany.

World's Top Tourist Countries
Number of international visitors, in millions

Country	Visitors
France	81.9
Spain	59.2
USA	56.0
China	54.7
Italy	43.7

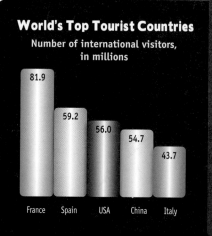

235

World's Most Visited City

ORLANDO

Approximately 47.1 million people visited Orlando, Florida in 2008. About 94% of visitors are from the United States, and some 77% of them are on vacation. International travelers, accounting for about 6% of visitors, are most commonly from the United Kingdom. Some of the main attractions in Orlando are Walt Disney World, Universal Studios, and Sea World. Each year visitors spend about $30 billion in the city, and the tourism industry accounts for about 24% of area jobs.

World's Most Visited Cities

Number of annual visitors, in millions

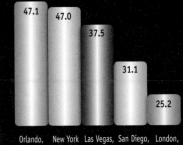

Orlando, USA	New York City, USA	Las Vegas, USA	San Diego, USA	London, UK
47.1	47.0	37.5	31.1	25.2

United States' Most Visited National Site
BLUE RIDGE PARKWAY

Each year more than 17 million people travel to North Carolina and Virginia to visit the Blue Ridge Parkway. The Blue Ridge is part of the eastern Appalachian Mountains and has an average elevation of 3,000 feet (914 m). The 469-mile (755 km) stretch of road winds through four national forests. Construction began on the country's first scenic parkway in 1935, and was completed in 1987. Some of the most popular activities along the Blue Ridge Parkway include hiking, camping, bicycling, and photographing nature.

United States' Most Visited National Sites

Number of annual visitors, in millions

Site	Visitors
Blue Ridge Parkway, North Carolina–Virginia	16.31
Golden Gate National Recreation Area, California	14.55
Gateway National Recreation Area, New Jersey–New York	9.43
Great Smoky Mountains, Tennessee–North Carolina	9.04
Lake Mead National Recreation Area, Arizona–Nevada	7.60

ENTERING
BLUE RIDGE PARKWAY

NATIONAL PARK SERVICE
UNITED STATES DEPARTMENT OF THE INTERIOR

Country with the Most Airports

UNITED STATES

There are 14,947 airports located in the United States. That is more than the number of airports for the other nine top countries combined. The top two busiest airports in the world are also located in the United States. All together, US airports serve more than 716 million domestic travelers a year. With the threat of terrorism and the state of the economy, the airline industry lost $10 billion in 2002. In September 2005, rising fuel costs and competition from discount airlines caused several major airlines to file for bankruptcy. After a brief rise in profits in 2007, the industry's earnings fell again in 2008 due to the slow economy and high fuel costs.

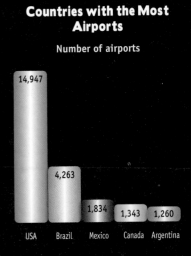

Countries with the Most Airports

Number of airports

USA	Brazil	Mexico	Canada	Argentina
14,947	4,263	1,834	1,343	1,260

World's Busiest Airport

HARTSFIELD-JACKSON ATLANTA INTERNATIONAL AIRPORT

The Hartsfield-Jackson Atlanta International Airport serves more than 89 million travelers in one year. That's more people than are living in California, Texas, and Florida combined. Approximately 994,350 planes depart and arrive at this airport every year. With parking lots, runways, maintenance facilities, and other buildings, the Hartsfield terminal complex covers about 130 acres (53 ha). Hartsfield-Jackson Atlanta International Airport has a north and a south terminal, an underground train, and six concourses with a total of 154 domestic and 28 international gates.

World's Busiest Airports
Number of annual passengers, in millions

Hartsfield-Jackson Atlanta Intl., USA	Chicago O'Hare Intl., USA	Heathrow Intl., UK	Haneda Intl., Japan	Los Angeles Intl., USA
89.3	76.1	68.0	66.8	61.8

World's Busiest Airline

SOUTHWEST AIRLINES

When travelers took to the skies in 2008, 101.9 million of them chose to fly Southwest Airlines. The company flies to 67 U.S. cites, with approximately 3,300 flights a day. With a fleet of 500 Boeing 737 planes—each an average of about 9 years old—Southwest also has some of the newest planes in the industry. The company was founded in 1971 and only offered service within Texas. By 1982, service was expanded to major cities throughout the country, including San Francisco, Los Angeles, and Phoenix. Today, Southwest employs more than 35,000 people throughout the country.

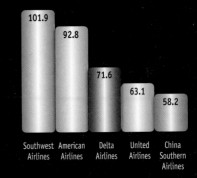

World's Busiest Airlines

Number of annual passengers, in millions

Southwest Airlines	American Airlines	Delta Airlines	United Airlines	China Southern Airlines
101.9	92.8	71.6	63.1	58.2

Country that Produces the Most Cars

JAPAN

Japan produced close to 10 million cars in 2008—that's almost enough to give every man, woman, and child living in Michigan one vehicle. Japan began producing cars in the early 1900s, and became the world's top producer by 2000. The country has about twelve main automakers, including Toyota, Honda, Nissan, Mitsubishi, Subaru, and Isuzu. Japan also lays claim to the world's bestselling car—the Toyota Camry—which has held that title for several years. However, with the economic crisis worsening in 2009, Japan—along with many other countries—has cut auto jobs and slowed production to save money.

Countries that Produce the Most Cars

Number of cars produced annually, in millions

Country	Cars produced (millions)
Japan	9.94
China	6.38
Germany	5.70
USA	3.92
South Korea	3.72

Times Sq-42 St Station
S N Q R W
1 2 3 7
♿Elevator to N Q R W at 42 St
For A C E enter at 8 Avenue

Enter with or buy MetroCard
6am-12 midnight or see
agent at 42 St & 7 Av

City with the Longest Subway System

NEW YORK CITY

The New York subway system consists of 660 miles (1,062.2 km) of track—more than enough to run from the Big Apple to Louisville, Kentucky. An additional 182 miles (292.9 km) of track lie beneath the city streets, but they are not currently in use. New York City has 468 subway stations, which is just 35 fewer than the number of all other US stations combined. There are approximately 6,200 subway cars in use, and together they travel about 353.7 million miles (569.2 million km) annually. The New York City subway system opened in 1904 with 9 miles (14.5 km) of track and charged just five cents per ride.

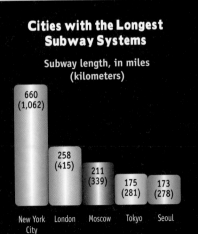

Cities with the Longest Subway Systems

Subway length, in miles (kilometers)

New York City	London	Moscow	Tokyo	Seoul
660 (1,062)	258 (415)	211 (339)	175 (281)	173 (278)

City with the Busiest Subway System

TOKYO

Every year, more than 3 billion riders pack into the Tokyo subway. The system operates more than 2,500 cars and 282 subway stations. The tracks run for 175 miles (281 km). The Tokyo Underground Railroad opened in 1927. It has expanded through the years to include nine subway lines that connect the bustling areas of Chiyoda, Minato, and Chuo. The Tokyo Metro has recently taken steps to upgrade its cars and stations, reinforcing car frames and redesigning station platforms.

Cities with the Busiest Subway Systems

Number of passengers per year, in billions

Tokyo	Moscow	Seoul	New York City	Mexico City
3.01	2.52	1.65	1.56	1.41

244

Country with the Most Vehicles

UNITED STATES

With more than 244 million vehicles registered in the United States, America outnumbers every country in the world in vehicle ownership. There are 136.5 million cars, 107.9 million trucks, and 822,000 buses. There are approximately 478 cars per 1,000 people throughout the country. More than 91 percent of all US residents have access to motor vehicles. With 33.2 million cars, California is the state with the most registered automobiles in the nation. The average American driver spends about 21 hours each year stuck in traffic.

Countries with the Most Vehicles

Number of vehicles, in millions

Country	Vehicles
USA	244.2
Japan	86.2
Germany	54.5
Italy	38.6
France	37.8

US
RECORDS

Alabama to Wyoming

State with the Oldest Mardi Gras

ALABAMA

People in Mobile, Alabama, have been celebrating Mardi Gras since 1703, although they did not have an official parade event until 1831. After a brief hiatus during the Civil War, the celebrations started back up in 1866 and have been growing ever since. Today, some 100,000 people gather in Mobile to enjoy the 22 parades that take place during the two weeks that lead up to Mardi Gras. On the biggest day—Fat Tuesday—six parades wind through the downtown waterfront, with floats and costumed dancers. But at the stroke of midnight, the partying stops and plans for the next year begin.

246

United States' Oldest Mardi Gras Celebrations

Number of years since celebration began*

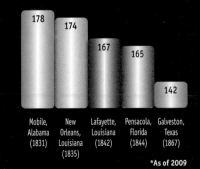

Mobile, Alabama (1831)	New Orleans, Louisiana (1835)	Lafayette, Louisiana (1842)	Pensacola, Florida (1844)	Galveston, Texas (1867)
178	174	167	165	142

*As of 2009

State with the Largest National Forest

ALASKA

The Tongass National Forest covers approximately 17,450,578 acres (7,061,998 ha) in southeast Alaska. That's about the same size as West Virginia. It is also home to the world's largest temperate rain forest. Some of the forest's trees are more than 700 years old. About 11,000 miles (17,703 km) of shoreline are inside the park. Some of the animals that live in the forest include bears, salmon, and wolves. The world's largest concentration of bald eagles also spend the fall and winter here on the Chilkat River.

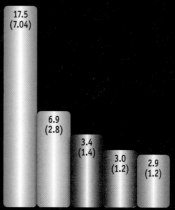

United States' Largest National Forests

Size, in millions of acres (hectares)

Forest	Size
Tongass National Forest, Alaska	17.5 (7.04)
Chugach National Forest, Alaska	6.9 (2.8)
Toiyabe National Forest, Nevada	3.4 (1.4)
Tonto National Forest, Arizona	3.0 (1.2)
Boise National Forest, Idaho	2.9 (1.2)

State with the Largest Collection of Telescopes

ARIZONA

The Kitt Peak National Observatory is home to 26 different telescopes—24 optical telescopes and 2 radio telescopes. Located above the Sonora Desert, the site was chosen to house the collection of equipment because of its clear weather, low relative humidity, and steady atmosphere. Eight different astronomical research institutions maintain and operate the telescopes. The observatory is overseen by the National Optical Astronomy Observatories. One of the most prominent telescopes housed at Kitt Peak is the McMath-Pierce Solar Telescope, the second-largest solar telescope in the world.

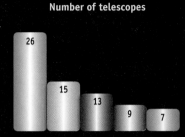

United States' Largest Collections of Telescopes

Number of telescopes

Kitt Peak National Observatory, Arizona	Custer Institute, New York	Mauna Kea, Hawaii	Stull Observatory, New York	Lick Observatory, California
26	15	13	9	7

State with the Largest Retail Headquarters

ARKANSAS

Wal-Mart—headquartered in Bentonville, Arkansas—logged $405.6 billion in sales in 2008. The company was founded in 1962 by Arkansas native Sam Walton, who saw his small variety stores grow into giant grocery stores, membership warehouse clubs, and deep-discount warehouse outlets. Walton's original store in Bentonville now serves as the company's visitor center. Each year, the company gives back some of what it earns to more than 100,000 charitable and community-based organizations.

United States' Largest Retail Headquarters

2008 sales, in billions of US dollars

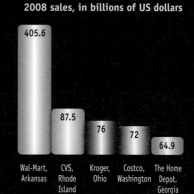

Wal-Mart, Arkansas	CVS, Rhode Island	Kroger, Ohio	Costco, Washington	The Home Depot, Georgia
405.6	87.5	76	72	64.9

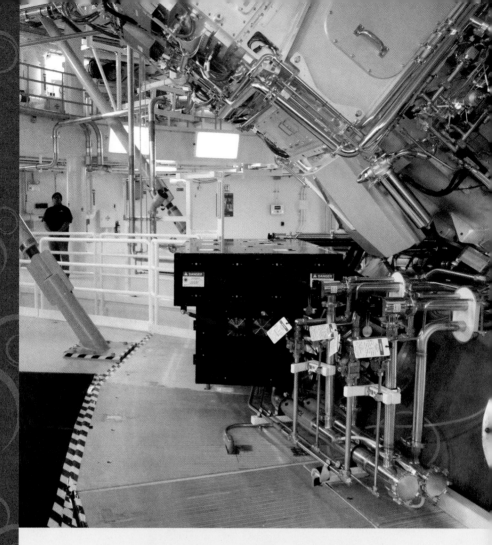

State with the World's Largest Laser

CALIFORNIA

The National Ignition Facility in California is home to the NIF laser—the largest laser in the world, weighing 264,000 pounds (119,748 kg) and featuring a target chamber with a 32.8-foot (10 meter) diameter. The NIF laser consists of 192 laser beams that can collectively focus on a tiny spot within the target chamber, creating a temperature of 100 million degrees. That's about 60 times more powerful than the next most powerful laser. This will help scientists research new ways to create energy in the future. The giant complex that houses the laser is approximately the size of three football fields.

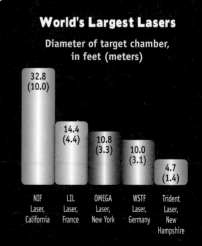

World's Largest Lasers

Diameter of target chamber, in feet (meters)

32.8 (10.0)	14.4 (4.4)	10.8 (3.3)	10.0 (3.1)	4.7 (1.4)
NIF Laser, California	LIL Laser, France	OMEGA Laser, New York	WSTF Laser, Germany	Trident Laser, New Hampshire

State's Baseball Team with the Highest Seasonal Attendance

COLORADO

In 1993, the seasonal attendance for the Colorado Rockies was an impressive 4.48 million fans. The Rockies finished up their inaugural season in October of the same year with the most wins by a National League expansion team. The Rockies played at Mile High Stadium for their first two years. The team moved to Denver's Coors Field in 1995. The new park was designed to have 43,800 seats, but with such high attendance at Mile High Stadium, architects reworked the plans to include 50,200 seats. The team proceeded to sell out 203 consecutive games.

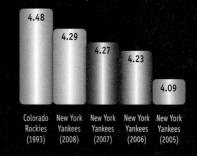

Baseball Teams with the Highest Seasonal Attendance

Seasonal attendance, in millions

Colorado Rockies (1993)	New York Yankees (2008)	New York Yankees (2007)	New York Yankees (2006)	New York Yankees (2005)
4.48	4.29	4.27	4.23	4.09

State with the Oldest Theme Park

CONNECTICUT

Lake Compounce in Bristol, Connecticut, first opened as a picnic park in 1846. The park's first electric roller coaster, the Green Dragon, was introduced in 1914 and cost ten cents per ride. It was replaced by the WildCat in 1927, and the wooden coaster still operates today. In 1996 the park got a $50 million upgrade, which included the thrilling new roller coaster Boulder Dash. It is the only coaster to be built into a mountainside. Another $3.3 million was spent on upgrades in 2005, including an 800-foot (244 m) lazy river.

252

United States' Oldest Theme Parks

Number of years open*

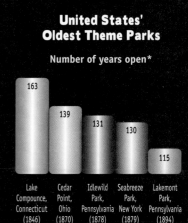

163	139	131	130	115
Lake Compounce, Connecticut (1846)	Cedar Point, Ohio (1870)	Idlewild Park, Pennsylvania (1878)	Seabreeze Park, New York (1879)	Lakemont Park, Pennsylvania (1894)

*As of 2009

State with the Largest Pumpkin-Throwing Contest

DELAWARE

Each year approximately 28,000 people gather in Sussex County, Delaware, for the annual World Championship Punkin Chunkin. More than 60 teams compete during the three-day festival to see who can chuck their pumpkin the farthest. Each team constructs a machine that has a mechanical or compressed-air firing device—no explosives are allowed. The farthest a pumpkin has traveled during the championship is 4,434 feet (1,352 m), or the length of twelve football fields. The total combined distance of all the pumpkins chunked at the 2007 championship totaled almost 12 miles (19 km). Each year the festival raises about $100,000 and benefits St. Jude Children's Hospital.

United States' Largest Pumpkin-Throwing Contests

Number of spectators

Millsboro, Delaware	Morton, Illinois	York, Pennsylvania	Busti, New York	Salina, Kansas
28,000	4,000	3,000	2,500	1,500

State with the Most Lightning Strikes

FLORIDA

Southern Florida is known as the Lightning Capital of the United States, with 26.3 bolts occurring over each square mile (2.6 sq km)—the equivalent of 10 city blocks—each year. Some 70 percent of all strikes occur between noon and 6:00 p.m., and the most dangerous months are July and August. Most lightning bolts measure 2 to 3 miles (5.2 to 7.8 km) long and can generate between 100 million and 1 billion volts of electricity. The air in a lightning bolt is heated to 50,000°F (27,760°C).

States with the Most Lightning Strikes

Annual bolts per square mile (2.6 sq km)

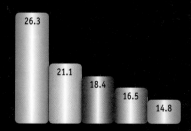

Florida	Louisiana	Mississippi	Alabama	South Carolina
26.3	21.1	18.4	16.5	14.8

State with the Largest Sports Hall of Fame

GEORGIA

The Georgia Sports Hall of Fame fills 43,000 square feet (3,995 sq m) with memorabilia from Georgia's most accomplished college, amateur, and professional athletes. Some 230,000 bricks, 245 tons (222 t) of steel, and 7,591 pounds (3,443 kg) of glass were used in its construction. The hall owns more than 3,000 artifacts and displays about 1,000 of them at a time. Some Hall of Famers include baseball legend Hank Aaron, Olympic basketball great Theresa Edwards, and Super Bowl I champion Bill Curry.

United States' Largest Sports Halls of Fame

Area, in square feet (square meters)

Georgia Sports Hall of Fame	Alabama Sports Hall of Fame	Virginia Sports Hall of Fame	Mississippi Sports Hall of Fame	Kansas Sports Hall of Fame
43,000 (3,995)	33,000 (3,066)	32,000 (3,000)	21,542 (2,001)	20,000 (1,900)

255

State with the Largest Submillimeter Wavelength Telescope

HAWAII

Mauna Kea—located on the island of Hawaii— is home to the world's largest submillimeter wavelength telescope, with a diameter of 49 feet (15 m). The James Clerk Maxwell Telescope (JCMT) is used to study our solar system, interstellar dust and gas, and distant galaxies. Mauna Kea also houses one of the world's largest optical/infrared (Keck I and II) and dedicated infrared (UKIRT) telescopes in the world. Mauna Kea is an ideal spot for astronomy because the atmosphere above the dormant volcano is very dry with little cloud cover, and its distance from city lights ensures a clear night sky.

World's Largest Submillimeter Wavelength Telescopes

Diameter of lens, in feet (meters)

James Clerk Maxwell Telescope (JCMT), Hawaii	Caltech Submillimeter Observatory (CSO), Hawaii	Atacama Submillimeter Telescope (ASTE), Chile	Heinrich Hertz Telescope (HHT), Arizona	Submillimeter Telescope (SMT), Arizona
49 (15)	34.0 (10.4)	32.8 (10)	32.8 (10)	32.8 (10)

State with the Largest Human-Made Geyser

IDAHO

The man-made geyser located in Soda Springs, Idaho, shoots water 150 feet (45.7 m) into the air. The geyser was created in November 1937 when people were searching for a hot water source for a thermal-heated swimming pool. The drill dug down about 315 feet (96.0 m) before it hit water. The pressure—created as water mixes with carbon dioxide gas—causes the water to shoot into the air. The Soda Springs geyser is now capped and controlled by a timer programmed to erupt every hour.

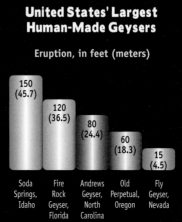

United States' Largest Human-Made Geysers

Eruption, in feet (meters)

Soda Springs, Idaho	Fire Rock Geyser, Florida	Andrews Geyser, North Carolina	Old Perpetual, Oregon	Fly Geyser, Nevada
150 (45.7)	120 (36.5)	80 (24.4)	60 (18.3)	15 (4.5)

257

State with the Largest Cookie Factory

ILLINOIS

The Nabisco factory covers 46 acres (18.6 ha) on South Kedzie Avenue in Chicago, Illinois. The 1.75 million-square-foot (162,000 sq m) cookie factory is also one of the largest bakeries in the world. The Nabisco plant employs about 2,000 workers, and they produce about 320 million pounds (145 million kg) of Oreo cookies, Fig Newtons, and Ritz crackers each year. The factory has storage capacity for 8.5 million pounds (3.9 million kg) of flour, 2.4 million pounds (1.1 million kg) of sugar, and 1.5 million pounds (680,388 kg) of vegetable oil. There are also 20 ovens in the facility that each measure about 300 feet (91 m) in length.

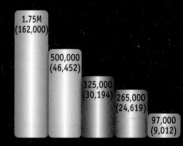

United States' Largest Cookie Factories

Area, in square feet (square meters)

- Nabisco, Illinois: 1.75M (162,000)
- Entenmann's, New York: 500,000 (46,452)
- Interstate Bakeries Corporation, Missouri: 325,000 (30,194)
- Pepperidge Farm, Connecticut: 265,000 (24,619)
- Otis Spunkmeyer, Texas: 97,000 (9,012)

State with the Largest Half Marathon

INDIANA

Cars aren't the only things racing in Indianapolis, Indiana. Each May some 35,000 runners take part in the Indianapolis Life 500 Festival Mini-Marathon. This makes the mini-marathon the nation's largest half marathon and the nation's eighth-longest road race. The 13.1-mile (21.1 km) race winds through downtown and includes a lap along the Indianapolis Motor Speedway oval. About 100 musical groups entertain the runners as they complete the course. A giant pasta dinner and after-race party await the runners at the end of the day. The mini-marathon is part of a weekend celebration that centers around the Indianapolis 500 auto race.

United States' Largest Half Marathons

Number of runners

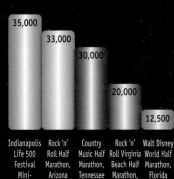

Indianapolis Life 500 Festival Mini-Marathon, Indiana	35,000
Rock 'n' Roll Half Marathon, Arizona	33,000
Country Music Half Marathon, Tennessee	30,000
Rock 'n' Roll Virginia Beach Half Marathon, Virginia	20,000
Walt Disney World Half Marathon, Florida	12,500

State with the Highest Egg Production

IOWA

Iowa tops all other states in the country in egg production, turning out approximately 14.4 billion eggs per year. That's enough to give every person in the United States about three and a half dozen eggs each! That's a good thing, because each person in America eats about 256 eggs per year. The state has 53 million laying hens, and each is capable of laying about 269 eggs a year. These hungry hens eat about 55 million bushels of corn and 27.5 million bushels of soybeans annually. In addition to selling the eggs as they are, Iowa's processing plants turn them into frozen, liquid, dried, or specialty egg products.

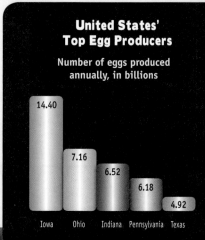

**United States'
Top Egg Producers**

Number of eggs produced
annually, in billions

Iowa	Ohio	Indiana	Pennsylvania	Texas
14.40	7.16	6.52	6.18	4.92

State with the Windiest City

KANSAS

According to average annual wind speeds collected by the National Climatic Data Center, Dodge City, Kansas, is the windiest city in the United States, with an average wind speed of 14 miles (22.5 km) per hour. Located in Ford County, the city borders the Santa Fe Trail and is rich in history. The city was established in 1872 and had a reputation as a tough cowboy town. With help from legendary sheriffs like Wyatt Earp, order was restored and the town grew steadily. Today tourists come to take in the area's history.

United States' Windiest Cities

Average wind speed, in miles (kilometers) per hour

Dodge City, Kansas	Amarillo, Texas	Rochester, Minnesota	Cheyenne, Wyoming	Kahului, Hawaii
14.0 (22.5)	13.5 (21.7)	12.9 (20.7)	12.9 (20.7)	12.8 (20.6)

State with the Largest Fireworks Display

KENTUCKY

Thunder Over Louisville is North America's largest fireworks display, drawing approximately 800,000 spectators each year. It is the opening ceremony for the Kentucky Derby Festival. Eight 400-foot (122 m) barges line both sides of the Second Street Bridge and serve as a stage for the 26-minute show. During the show, some 60 tons (54 t) of fireworks shells and 250 tons (227 t) of launching tubes are used. The show is set to all types of music, ranging from rock and roll to Broadway tunes. Millions of people worldwide also see the show when it's rebroadcast to 150 countries on the Fourth of July.

United States' Largest Fireworks Displays

Number of fireworks shells used

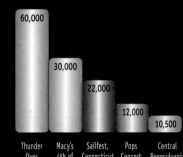

60,000	30,000	22,000	12,000	10,500
Thunder Over Louisville, Kentucky	Macy's 4th of July, New York	Sailfest, Connecticut	Pops Concert at the Esplanade, Massachusetts	Central Pennsylvania 4th Fest, Pennsylvania

State with the Largest Alligator Population

LOUISIANA

There are approximately 1.5 million alligators living in Louisiana. About 1 million alligators live in the wild, and another half million are raised on farms. In 1986, Louisiana began an alligator ranching business, which encourages farmers to raise thousands of the reptiles each year. The farmers must return some alligators to the wild, but they are allowed to sell the rest for profit. The released alligators have an excellent chance of thriving in the wild because they have been well fed and are a good size. Although alligators can be found in the state's bayous, swamps, and ponds, most live in Louisiana's 3 million acres (1.2 million ha) of coastal marshland.

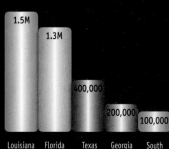

States with the Largest Alligator Populations

Total number of alligators

Louisiana	Florida	Texas	Georgia	South Carolina
1.5M	1.3M	400,000	200,000	100,000

263

State with the Oldest State Fair

MAINE

The first Skowhegan State Fair took place in 1819—a year before Maine officially became a state! The fair took place in January, and hundreds of people came despite the harsh weather. Originally sponsored by the Somerset Central Agricultural Society, the fair name became official in 1842. State fairs were very important in the early 1900s. With no agricultural colleges in existence, fairs became the best way for farmers to learn about new agricultural methods and equipment. Today the Skowhegan State Fair features more than 7,000 exhibitors who compete for prize money totaling more than $200,000. The fair also includes a demolition derby, a children's barnyard, concerts, livestock exhibits, and arts and crafts.

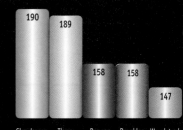

**United States'
Oldest State Fairs**

Number of years since fair first held*

190	189	158	158	147
Skowhegan State Fair, Maine (1819)	Three County Fair, Massachusetts (1820)	Bangor State Fair, Maine (1851)	Brooklyn Fair, Connecticut (1851)	Woodstock Fair, Vermont (1862)

*As of 2009

State with the Oldest Airport

MARYLAND

The Wright brothers founded College Park Airport in 1909 to teach Army officers how to fly, and it has been in operation ever since. The airport is now owned by the Maryland-National Capital Park and Planning Commission and is on the Register of Historic Places. Many aviation "firsts" occurred at this airport, such as the first woman passenger in the United States (1909), the first test of a bomb-dropping device (1911), and the first US airmail service (1918). The College Park Aviation Museum is located on its grounds, and it exhibits aviation memorabilia.

United States' Oldest Airports

Number of years open*

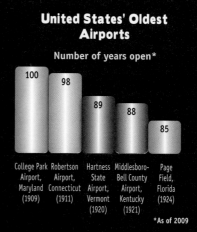

College Park Airport, Maryland (1909)	Robertson Airport, Connecticut (1911)	Hartness State Airport, Vermont (1920)	Middlesboro-Bell County Airport, Kentucky (1921)	Page Field, Florida (1924)
100	98	89	88	85

*As of 2009

265

State with the Oldest Baseball Stadium

MASSACHUSETTS

Fenway Park opened its doors to Massachusetts baseball fans on April 20, 1912. The Boston Red Sox—the park's home team—won the World Series that year. The park celebrated in 2004 when the Sox won the World Series again. The park is also the home of the Green Monster—a giant 37-foot (11.3 m) wall with an additional 23-foot (7 m) screen that has plagued home-run hitters since the park first opened. The park's unique dimensions were not intended to prevent home runs, however; they were meant to keep nonpaying fans outside. A seat out in the right-field bleachers is painted red to mark where the longest measurable home run hit inside the park landed. It measured 502 feet (153 m) and was hit by Ted Williams in 1946. Some of the other baseball legends who played at Fenway include Cy Young, Babe Ruth, Jimmie Fox, and Carlton Fisk.

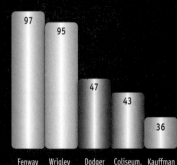

United States' Oldest Baseball Stadiums

Number of years open*

Fenway Park, Boston (1912)	Wrigley Field, Chicago (1914)	Dodger Stadium, Los Angeles (1962)	Coliseum, Oakland (1966)	Kauffman Stadium, Kansas City (1973)
97	95	47	43	36

*As of 2009

BOSTON RED SOX

State with the Largest Indoor Waterfall
MICHIGAN

The 114-foot (34.7 m) waterfall located in the lobby of the International Center in Detroit, Michigan, is the tallest indoor waterfall in the world. The backdrop of this impressive waterfall is a 9,000-square-foot (840 sq m) slab of marble that was imported from the Greek island of Tinos and installed by eight marble craftsmen. About 6,000 gallons (27,276 L) of water spill down the waterfall each minute. That's the equivalent of 80,000 cans of soda! Visitors can see this $1.5 million creation as they stroll through the International Center, which also houses many retail shops. Located in the historic Trappers Alley in the Greektown section of the city, the eight-story building was formerly used as a seed warehouse.

World's Largest Indoor Waterfalls

Height, in feet (meters)

Location	Height
International Center, Michigan	114 (34.7)
Trump Tower, New York	90 (27.4)
Orchid Hotel, India	70 (21.3)
Casino Windsor, Michigan	60 (18.3)
Mohegan Sun, Connecticut	55 (16.8)

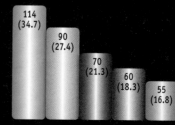

State with the Largest Indoor Theme Park

MINNESOTA

Nickelodeon Universe is located inside the Mall of America in Bloomington, Minnesota, and covers 7 acres (2.8 ha). The park offers 30 rides, including the Xcel Energy Log Chute, SpongeBob Square- Pants Rock Bottom Plunge, Splat-O-Sphere, Skyscraper Ferris wheel, Timber Twister roller coaster, Mighty Axe, and Avatar Airbender. Some of the other attractions at the park are a rock-climbing wall, petting zoo, and game arcade. Kids can also meet Dora, Diego, Blue, and SpongeBob.

268

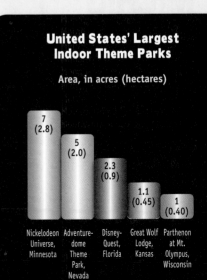

United States' Largest Indoor Theme Parks

Area, in acres (hectares)

7 (2.8)	5 (2.0)	2.3 (0.9)	1.1 (0.45)	1 (0.40)
Nickelodeon Universe, Minnesota	Adventure-dome Theme Park, Nevada	Disney-Quest, Florida	Great Wolf Lodge, Kansas	Parthenon at Mt. Olympus, Wisconsin

State with the Most Catfish

MISSISSIPPI

There are more than 530 million catfish in Mississippi—more than 55 percent of the world's farm-raised supply. That's almost enough to give every person in the state 235 fish each. Mississippi's catfish crop is worth about $218 million annually. There are about 360 catfish producers farming 100,000 water acres (40,468 ha). The state's residents are quite proud of their successful fish industry and celebrate at the World Catfish Festival in Belzoni.

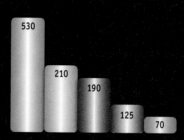

States with the Most Catfish

Number of catfish, in millions

Mississippi	Louisiana	Alabama	Arkansas	Texas
530	210	190	125	70

State with the Largest Outdoor Theater

MISSOURI

The Municipal Theatre in St. Louis, Missouri—affectionately known as the Muny—is the nation's largest outdoor theater, with 80,000 square feet (7,432 sq m) and 11,500 seats—about the same size as a regulation soccer field. Amazingly, construction on the giant theater was completed in just 42 days at a cost of $10,000. The theater opened in 1917 with a production of Verdi's *Aïda*, and the best seats cost only $1.00. The Muny offers classic Broadway shows each summer, with past productions including *The King and I*, *The Wizard of Oz*, and *Oliver!* The last nine rows of the theater are always held as free seats for the public, just as they have been since the Muny opened.

United States' Largest Outdoor Theaters

Area, in square feet (square meters)

Muny, Missouri	Alpine Valley Music Theater, Wisconsin	Journal Pavilion, New Mexico	Miller Outdoor Theater, Texas	Starlight Theater, Missouri
80,000 (7,432)	55,000 (5,100)	45,000 (4,200)	37,000 (3,500)	12,000 (1,100)

State with the Largest Bighorn Sheep Population

MONTANA

With a population of 6,100 bighorn sheep, Montana has more of these wild endangered mammals than any other state. The population has quadrupled in the last 60 years. Many of Montana's bighorn sheep live in an area known as the Rocky Mountain Front—a 100-mile (160.9 km) area that stretches from Glacier National Park to the town of Lincoln. A ram's horns can weigh up to 30 pounds (13.6 kg)—more than all of the bones in its body. Rams use these giant horns when they butt heads with a rival sheep, and can hit each other at up to 20 miles (32.2 km) per hour.

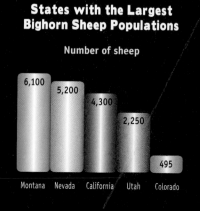

States with the Largest Bighorn Sheep Populations

Number of sheep

Montana	Nevada	California	Utah	Colorado
6,100	5,200	4,300	2,250	495

271

State with the Largest Hailstone

NEBRASKA

During a severe thunderstorm on June 22, 2003, the small town of Aurora, Nebraska, was pounded with a hailstone that measured at least 7 inches (17.8 cm) in diameter and had a circumference of 18.8 inches (47.7 cm). That's about the same size as a soccer ball. Scientists think that the hailstone was probably even bigger, but had melted some before it was preserved in a freezer. Hailstones of this size can fall at a speed of 100 miles (161 km) an hour. Sometimes hailstones can contain other objects, such as rocks, insects, and leaves.

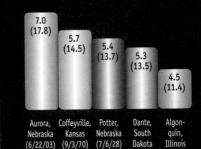

United States' Largest Hailstones

Diameter, in inches (centimeters)

Aurora, Nebraska (6/22/03)	Coffeyville, Kansas (9/3/70)	Potter, Nebraska (7/6/28)	Dante, South Dakota (8/21/07)	Algonquin, Illinois (6/20/08)
7.0 (17.8)	5.7 (14.5)	5.4 (13.7)	5.3 (13.5)	4.5 (11.4)

State with the Largest Glass Sculpture

NEVADA

Fiori di Como—the breathtaking chandelier at the Bellagio Hotel in Las Vegas, Nevada—measures 65.7 feet by 29.5 feet (20 m by 9 m). Created by Dale Chihuly, the handblown glass chandelier consists of more than 2,000 discs of colored glass. Each disc is about 18 inches (45.7 cm) wide and hangs about 20 feet (6.1 m) overhead. Together, these colorful discs look like a giant field of flowers. The chandelier required about 10,000 pounds (4,536 kg) of steel and 40,000 pounds (18,144 kg) of handblown glass. The sculpture's name translates to "Flowers of Como." The Bellagio was modeled after the hotel on Lake Como in Italy.

United States' Largest Glass Sculptures

Length, in feet (meters)

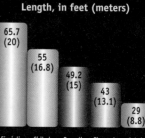

65.7 (20)	55 (16.8)	49.2 (15)	43 (13.1)	29 (8.8)
Fiori di Como, Nevada	Chihuly Tower, Oklahoma	Borealis, Michigan	Fireworks of Glass, Indiana	Cobalt Blue Chandelier, Washington

273

State with the Oldest Post Office

NEW HAMPSHIRE

Predating the Pony Express, the Hinsdale post office in New Hampshire opened its doors in 1816, and has been in operation ever since. The mail was delivered by horse and wagon, there were no paved roads, and it only cost a few pennies to send a letter. In the mid-1800s, nearby Brattleboro, Vermont, was connected to the railroad, and mail was moved by train. In 1905, the first rural route was in place and mail was delivered to some homes by horse and buggy. Today the historic building is equipped with modern technology.

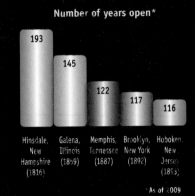

United States' Oldest Post Offices

Number of years open*

193	145	122	117	116
Hinsdale, New Hampshire (1816)	Galena, Illinois (1859)	Memphis, Tennessee (1887)	Brooklyn, New York (1892)	Hoboken, New Jersey (1893)

*As of 2009

State with the Longest Boardwalk

NEW JERSEY

The famous boardwalk in Atlantic City, New Jersey, stretches for 4 miles (6.4 km) along the beach. Combined with the adjoining boardwalk in Ventnor, the length increases to just under 6 miles (9.7 km). The 60-foot-wide (18 m) boardwalk opened on June 26, 1870. It was the first boardwalk built in the United States, and was designed to keep sand out of the tourists' shoes. Today the boardwalk is filled with amusement parks, shops, restaurants, and hotels. The boardwalk recently received a $100 million face-lift, which included new roofs, signs, and storefronts for surrounding buildings. About 37 million people take a stroll along the walk each year.

World's Longest Boardwalks

Length, in miles (kilometers)

Location	Length
Atlantic City, New Jersey	4.0 (6.4)
Coney Island, New York	3.0 (4.8)
FDR Boardwalk, New York	2.5 (4.0)
Corkscrew Swamp Sanctuary, Florida	2.3 (3.7)
Jarzoo Boardwalk, Sweden	2.0 (3.2)

275

State with the Largest Balloon Festival

NEW MEXICO

During the 2008 Kodak Albuquerque International Balloon Fiesta in New Mexico, approximately 500 hot-air and gas-filled balloons sailed across the sky. Held each October, the fiesta draws hundreds of thousands of spectators. This event attracts balloons from around the world, and is often seen in more than 50 countries. The festival takes place in the 365-acre (148 ha) Balloon Fiesta State Park. The Balloon Fiesta has also hosted some prestigious balloon races, including the Gordon Bennett Cup (1993), the World Gas Balloon Championship (1994), and the America's Challenge Gas Balloon Race (2006).

States with the Largest Balloon Festivals

Approximate number of balloons

Albuquerque, New Mexico	Gallup, New Mexico	Greenville, South Carolina	Colorado Springs, Colorado	Longview, Texas
500	200	150	100	80

State with the Longest Underwater Tunnel

NEW YORK

The Brooklyn-Battery Tunnel in New York measures 1.73 miles (2.78 km) long, making it the longest underwater tunnel in North America and the longest continuous underwater vehicular tunnel in the world. The tunnel passes under the East River and connects Battery Park in Manhattan with the Red Hook section of Brooklyn. It took 13,900 tons (12,609 t) of steel, about 205,000 cubic yards (156,700 cu m) of concrete, approximately 1,871 miles (3,011 km) of electrical wire, some 883,391 bolts, and 799,000 wall and ceiling tiles to build the tunnel. Completed in 1950, the $90 million tunnel carries about 60,000 vehicles a day.

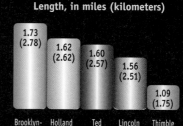

United States' Longest Underwater Tunnels

Length, in miles (kilometers)

Brooklyn-Battery Tunnel, New York	Holland Tunnel, New York	Ted Williams Tunnel, Massachusetts	Lincoln Tunnel, New York	Thimble Shoal Tunnel, Virginia
1.73 (2.78)	1.62 (2.62)	1.60 (2.57)	1.56 (2.51)	1.09 (1.75)

State that Grows the Most Sweet Potatoes

NORTH CAROLINA

North Carolina leads the country in sweet potato production, growing about 709.5 million pounds (321.8 kg) each year. This accounts for about 40 percent of the nation's sweet potato production. Farmers plant about 42,000 acres (16,997 ha) of sweet potato plants annually. In fact, the sweet potato is the official state vegetable of North Carolina. Oddly enough, these sweet veggies aren't really potatoes at all. Sweet potatoes are root plants—not tubers—and are actually part of the morning glory family.

278

States that Grow the Most Sweet Potatoes

Millions of pounds (kilograms) grown annually

State	Millions of pounds (kilograms)
North Carolina	709.5 (321.8)
California	425.6 (193.0)
Mississippi	350.0 (158.7)
Louisiana	282.5 (128.1)
Alabama	28.8 (13.0)

State with the Tallest Metal Sculpture

NORTH DAKOTA

In August 2001, Gary Greff created a 110-foot-tall (33.5 m) metal sculpture along the stretch of road between Gladstone and Regent, North Dakota. That's the height of an 11-story building! The 154-foot-wide (46.9 m) sculpture is called *Geese in Flight*, and shows Canada geese traveling across the prairie. Greff has created several other towering sculptures nearby, and the road has become known as the Enchanted Highway. He created these sculptures to attract tourists to the area and to support his hometown. He relies only on donations to finance his work.

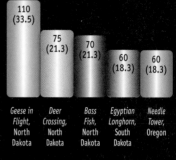

United States' Tallest Metal Sculptures

Height, in feet (meters)

110 (33.5)	75 (21.3)	70 (21.3)	60 (18.3)	60 (18.3)
Geese in Flight, North Dakota	Deer Crossing, North Dakota	Bass Fish, North Dakota	Egyptian Longhorn, South Dakota	Needle Tower, Oregon

State with the Largest Twins Gathering

OHIO

Each August, the town of Twinsburg, Ohio, hosts more than 4,000 twins at its annual Twins Day Festival. Both identical and fraternal twins from around the world participate, and many dress alike. The twins take part in games and contests, such as the oldest identical twins and the twins with the widest combined smile. There is also a "Double Take" parade, which is nationally televised. There are special twin programs for all age groups, since twins from ages 90 years to just 11 days old have attended. The event began in 1976 in honor of Aaron and Moses Wilcox, twin brothers who inspired the city to adopt its name in 1817.

World's Largest Twins Gatherings

Number of attendees

Twins Day Festival, Ohio	"Deux et plus" Gathering, France	Twins Weekend, Canada	Twins Plus Festival, Australia	Beijing Twins Festival, China
4,074	4,000	2,500	1,500	1,000

State with the Longest Multiple-Arch Dam

OKLAHOMA

With a length of 6,565 feet (2,001 m), the Pensacola Dam in Oklahoma is the world's longest multiple-arch dam. Built in 1940, the dam is located on the Grand River and contains the Grand Lake O' the Cherokees—one of the largest reservoirs in the country with 46,500 surface acres (18,818 ha) of water. The dam stands 145 feet (44 m) high. It was made out of 535,000 cubic yards of concrete, some 655,000 barrels of cement, another 10 million pounds (4.5 million kg) of structural steel, and 75,000 pounds (340,194 kg) of copper. The dam cost $27 million to complete.

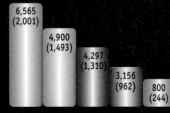

World's Longest Multiple-Arch Dams

Length, in feet (meters)

6,565 (2,001)	Pensacola Dam, Oklahoma
4,900 (1,493)	New Waddell Dam, Arizona
4,297 (1,310)	Daniel Johnson Dam, Canada
3,156 (962)	Florence Lake Dam, California
800 (244)	Mountain Dell Dam, Utah

281

State with the Deepest Lake

OREGON

At a depth of 1,932 feet (589 m), Crater Lake in southern Oregon partially fills the remains of an old volcanic basin. The crater was formed almost 7,700 years ago when Mount Mazama erupted and then collapsed. The lake averages about 5 miles (8 km) in diameter. Crater Lake National Park—the nation's fifth-oldest park—surrounds the majestic lake and measures 249 square miles (645 sq km). The area's large snowfalls average 530 inches (1,346 cm) a year, and supply Crater Lake with its water. In addition to being the United States' deepest lake, it's also the eighth-deepest lake in the world.

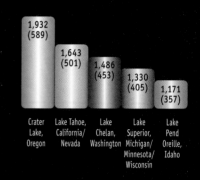

United States' Deepest Lakes

Greatest depth, in feet (meters)

Depth	Lake
1,932 (589)	Crater Lake, Oregon
1,643 (501)	Lake Tahoe, California/Nevada
1,486 (453)	Lake Chelan, Washington
1,330 (405)	Lake Superior, Michigan/Minnesota/Wisconsin
1,171 (357)	Lake Pend Oreille, Idaho

State with the Oldest Drive-in Theater

PENNSYLVANIA

Shankweiler's Drive-in Theater opened in 1934. It was the country's second drive-in theater, and is the oldest one still operating today. Located in Orefield, Pennsylvania, the single-screen theater can accommodate 320 cars. Approximately 90 percent of the theater's guests are children. Although they originally used sound boxes located beside the cars, today patrons can tune into a special radio station to hear the movies' music and dialogue. Shankweiler's is open from April to September.

United States' Oldest Drive-in Theaters

Number of years open*

Shank-weiler's Drive-in Theater, Pennsyl-vania (1934)	Lynn Auto Theatre, Ohio (1937)	Saco Drive-in, Maine (1939)	Hiway 50 Drive-in Theater, Tennessee (1946)	Sunset Drive-in Theater, Pennsyl-vania (1948)
75	72	70	63	61

*As of 2009

283

State with the Oldest Temple

RHODE ISLAND

The Touro Synagogue was dedicated during Hanukkah in December 1763 and is the oldest temple in the United States. Located in Newport, Rhode Island, the temple was designed by famous architect Peter Harrison and took four years to complete. In addition to serving as a symbol of religious freedom, the temple played another part in the country's history. When the British captured Newport in 1776, the temple briefly became a British hospital. Then, in 1781, George Washington met General Lafayette there to plan the final battles of the Revolution.

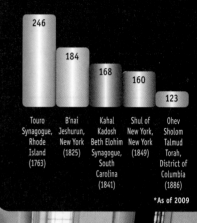

United States' Oldest Temples

Number of years since dedication

Touro Synagogue, Rhode Island (1763)	B'nai Jeshurun, New York (1825)	Kahal Kadosh Beth Elohim Synagogue, South Carolina (1841)	Shul of New York, New York (1849)	Ohev Sholom Talmud Torah, District of Columbia (1886)
246	184	168	160	123

*As of 2009

State with the Oldest Museum
SOUTH CAROLINA

The Charleston Museum in Charleston, South Carolina, was founded in 1773—three years before the Declaration of Independence was signed. The museum was founded to preserve the culture and history of the southern town and the surrounding area, and opened its doors to the public in 1824. Some of the exhibits found in the museum include furniture, silver, and art made in the area, as well as fossils of the birds and animals found there. Two historic houses, which were built between 1772 and 1803, are also run by the museum. Visitors can tour these homes to learn about the state's early architecture.

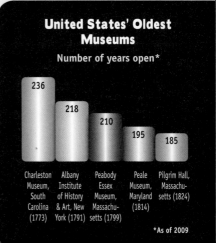

United States' Oldest Museums

Number of years open*

236	218	210	195	185
Charleston Museum, South Carolina (1773)	Albany Institute of History & Art, New York (1791)	Peabody Essex Museum, Massachusetts (1799)	Peale Museum, Maryland (1814)	Pilgrim Hall, Massachusetts (1824)

*As of 2009

State with the Largest Petrified Wood Collection

SOUTH DAKOTA

Lemmon's Petrified Wood Park in South Dakota is home to 30 acres (12.1 ha) of petrified wood. It covers an entire city block in downtown Lemmon. It was built between 1930 and 1932 when locals collected petrified wood from the area and constructed displays. One structure in the park—known as the Castle—weighs more than 300 tons (272 t) and is made partly from petrified wood and partly of petrified dinosaur and mammoth bones. Other exhibits include a wishing well, a waterfall, the Lemmon Pioneer Museum, and hundreds of pile sculptures.

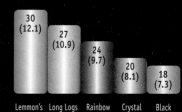

United States' Largest Petrified Wood Collections

Area, in acres (hectares)

Lemmon's Petrified Wood Park, South Dakota	Long Logs Forest, Arizona	Rainbow Forest, Arizona	Crystal Forest, Arizona	Black Forest, Arizona
30 (12.1)	27 (10.9)	24 (9.7)	20 (8.1)	18 (7.3)

State with the Largest Freshwater Aquarium

TENNESSEE

The Tennessee Aquarium in Chattanooga is an impressive 130,000 square feet (12,077 sq m), making it the largest freshwater aquarium in the world. The $45 million building holds a total of 400,000 gallons (1,514,165 L) of water. In addition, the aquarium features a 60,000-square-foot (5,574 sq m) building dedicated to the ocean and the creatures that live there. Permanent features in the aquarium include a discovery hall and an environmental learning lab. Some of the aquarium's 12,000 animals include baby alligators, paddlefish, lake sturgeon, sea dragons, and pipefish. And to feed all of these creatures, the aquarium goes through 12,000 crickets, 33,300 worms, and 1,200 pounds (545 kg) of seafood each month!

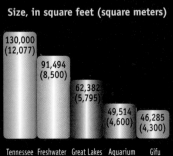

World's Largest Freshwater Aquariums

Size, in square feet (square meters)

130,000 (12,077)	91,494 (8,500)	62,382 (5,795)	49,514 (4,600)	46,285 (4,300)
Tennessee Aquarium, Tennessee	Freshwater Center, Denmark	Great Lakes Aquarium, Minnesota	Aquarium of the Lakes, Britain	Gifu Freshwater Aquarium, Japan

287

State with the Biggest Ferris Wheel

TEXAS

The State Fair of Texas boasts the nation's largest Ferris wheel. Called the Texas Star, this colossal wheel measures 212 feet (64.6 m) high. That's taller than a 20-story building! The Texas Star was built in Italy and shipped to Texas for its debut at the 1986 fair. Located in the 277-acre (112 ha) Fair Park, the Texas Star is just one of the 70 rides featured at the fair. The three-week-long State Fair of Texas is the biggest state fair in the country and brings in about $350 million in revenue annually. It is held in the fall, and the giant Ferris wheel is not the only grand-scale item there. Big Tex, a 52-foot-tall (15.9 m) cowboy, is the fair's mascot and the biggest cowboy in the United States.

288

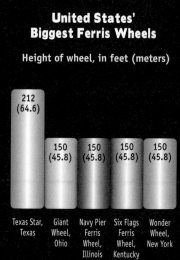

United States' Biggest Ferris Wheels

Height of wheel, in feet (meters)

Texas Star, Texas	Giant Wheel, Ohio	Navy Pier Ferris Wheel, Illinois	Six Flags Ferris Wheel, Kentucky	Wonder Wheel, New York
212 (64.6)	150 (45.8)	150 (45.8)	150 (45.8)	150 (45.8)

State with the City that Buys the Most Movies

UTAH

The residents of Salt Lake City, Utah, love to watch movies at home—about 73 percent of all households there buy at least one DVD each year. That's at least 132,670 purchases in a year. Some of the titles Salt Lake City residents bought probably included *The Dark Knight, Iron Man,* and *Alvin and the Chipmunks,* which were the three top-selling DVDs in the country in 2008. Residents of Utah's capital city might enjoy movies so much because so many are filmed there, including *High School Musical, Legally Blonde 2, Independence Day,* and *Dumb and Dumber.*

States with the Cities that Buy the Most Movies

Percentage of households that buy at least one DVD a year

Salt Lake City, Utah	Colorado Springs, Colorado	Columbus, Ohio	Las Vegas, Nevada	Newport News, Virginia
73	65	64	64	64

State that Produces the Most Maple Syrup

VERMONT

Maple syrup production in Vermont totaled 500,000 gallons (1,892,705 L) in 2008 and accounted for about 31 percent of the United States' total yield that year. There are about 2,000 maple syrup producers with 2.25 million tree taps in Vermont, and the annual production generates almost $13.1 million. It takes about five tree taps to collect enough maple sap—approximately 40 gallons (151.4 L)—to produce just 1 gallon (3.79 L) of syrup. Vermont maple syrup is also made into maple sugar, maple cream, and maple candies.

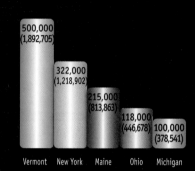

States that Produce the Most Maple Syrup

Production, in gallons (liters)

500,000 (1,892,705) — Vermont
322,000 (1,218,902) — New York
215,000 (813,863) — Maine
118,000 (446,678) — Ohio
100,000 (378,541) — Michigan

State with the Largest Office Building

VIRGINIA

The Pentagon Building in Arlington, Virginia, measures 6,636,360 square feet (616,538 sq m) and covers 583 acres (236 ha). In fact, the National Capitol can fit inside the building five times! Although the Pentagon contains 17.5 miles (28.2 km) of hallways, the design of the building allows people to reach any destination in about 7 minutes. The Pentagon is almost like a small city, employing about 23,000 people. About 200,000 phone calls are made there daily, and the internal post office handles about 1.2 million pieces of mail each month.

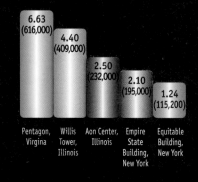

United States' Largest Office Buildings

Size, in millions of square feet (square meters)

Building	Size
Pentagon, Virgina	6.63 (616,000)
Willis Tower, Illinois	4.40 (409,000)
Aon Center, Illinois	2.50 (232,000)
Empire State Building, New York	2.10 (195,000)
Equitable Building, New York	1.24 (115,200)

State with the Longest Train Tunnel

WASHINGTON

The Cascade Tunnel runs through the Cascade Mountains in central Washington and measures almost 7.8 miles (12.6 km) long. The tunnel connects the towns of Berne and Scenic. It was built by the Great Northern Railway in 1929 to replace the original tunnel, which was built at an elevation frequently hit with snow slides. To help cool the trains' diesel engines and remove fumes, the tunnel is equipped with huge fans that blow air while and after a train passes.

United States' Longest Train Tunnels

Length, in miles (kilometers)

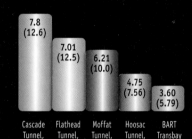

Cascade Tunnel, Washington	Flathead Tunnel, Missouri	Moffat Tunnel, Colorado	Hoosac Tunnel, Massachusetts	BART Transbay Tube, California
7.8 (12.6)	7.01 (12.5)	6.21 (10.0)	4.75 (7.56)	3.60 (5.79)

CASCADE TUNNEL
7.8 MILES LONG   ELEVATION 2247 FEET
41,152 FEET LONG   COMPLETED 1928

State with the World's Largest Teddy Bear

WEST VIRGINIA

In Charleston, West Virginia, the E.G. Bear Company created a giant patchwork teddy bear named Evan that measures 61 feet (18.6 m) tall. With an arm span of 25 feet (7.6 m), Evan could hug about 18 kids at one time. The company made the bear for an auction to benefit the Charleston Area Medical Center. The entire community helped to stuff the huge, cuddly creature in November 2008. Each person who volunteered received a bucket of stuffing and the opportunity to sign a wooden heart placed inside the bear.

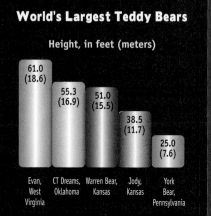

World's Largest Teddy Bears

Height, in feet (meters)

Evan, West Virginia	CT Dreams, Oklahoma	Warren Bear, Kansas	Jody, Kansas	York Bear, Pennsylvania
61.0 (18.6)	55.3 (16.9)	51.0 (15.5)	38.5 (11.7)	25.0 (7.6)

293

State with the Largest Water Park

WISCONSIN

Noah's Ark in Wisconsin Dells sprawls for 70 acres (28.4 ha) and includes 49 waterslides. One of the most popular—Dark Voyage—takes visitors on a twisting rapids ride in the dark. The ride can pump 8,000 gallons (30,283 L) of water a minute. Visitors can also enjoy two wave pools, two mile-long "endless" rivers, and four children's play areas. It takes 5 million gallons (19 million L) of water—the equivalent of more than 14 Olympic-size swimming pools—to fill all the pools and operate the 3 miles (4.8 km) of waterslides. Noah's Ark also boasts the country's longest watercoaster (Black Anaconda), the world's longest bowl ride (Time Warp), and the world's only 4D drive-in theater.

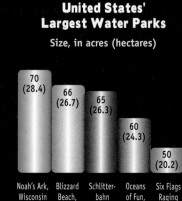

United States' Largest Water Parks

Size, in acres (hectares)

Noah's Ark, Wisconsin	Blizzard Beach, Florida	Schlitterbahn Waterpark Resort, Texas	Oceans of Fun, Missouri	Six Flags Raging Waters, California
70 (28.4)	66 (26.7)	65 (26.3)	60 (24.3)	50 (20.2)

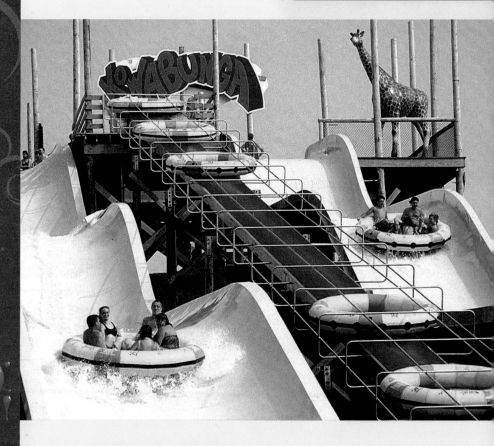

State with the Largest Coal Mine

WYOMING

North Antelope Rochelle Mine produces about 91.5 million tons (83 million t) of coal each year. Located near Gillette, Wyoming, the mine has produced more than 1 billion tons (907 million t) of coal since it first opened in 1983. The complex is the result of two mines—the North Antelope and the Rochelle Mine—combining in 1999. More than 1,000 people work there, mining the four giant pits in 12-hour shifts. The mine is owned by Peabody Energy, which produces enough coal to generate about 10 percent of the energy used in the United States and 2 percent of the energy used worldwide.

United States' Largest Coal Mines

Coal produced annually, in millions of tons (metric tons)

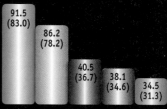

91.5 (83.0)	86.2 (78.2)	40.5 (36.7)	38.1 (34.6)	34.5 (31.3)
North Antelope Rochelle, Wyoming	Black Thunder, Wyoming	Cordero Mine, Wyoming	Jacobs Ranch Mine, Wyoming	Antelope Coal Mine, Wyoming

295

INDEX

301

303

PHOTO CREDITS ★

Pages 6-8, 10-20, 24, 26, 27, 32-36, 38-47, 49, 50, 53, 55, 57, 58, 62, 65, 72-74, 76-78, 62, 66, 80, 82, 83, 89, 90, 94, 95, 99-101, 103-105, 109, 113, 135, 158, 163, 218, 229, 238, 239, 241, 272: ©AP/Wide World; pages 9, 25, 37, 48, 52, 54, 59, 60, 61, 63, 64, 67, 68, 70, 71, 75, 79, 81, 84-87, 91, 93, 96-98, 102, 106, 108, 111, 112, 114-116, 132-134, 138, 139, 146-149, 154, 159, 164, 167, 172-177, 184, 185, 199, 201, 203-205, 217, 231, 234, 237, 240, 243, 246, 248, 251, 256, 258, 261-264, 266, 268, 269, 273, 275-277, 284, 286, 291, 295: ©Corbis; pages 21, 22, 28-31: ©Photofest; page 23: ©North Wind Picture Archive; page 25: ©istockphoto; pages 24, 107, 153, 236: ©Alamy Photos; pages 56, 110: ©Time, Inc.; page 88: ©Craig Blakenhorn/ FOX; page 92: ©Hulton Getty/Archive Photos; pages 119, 120, 126, 128, 129, 145, 151, 156, 157, 162, 165, 168, 170, 171, 173, 178, 179, 183, 186, 187, 190, 196, 197, 207, 209-213, 216, 219, 220, 225, 226, 232, 235-237, 242, 244, 247, 250, 254, 260, 271, 278, 282, 285, 289, 290, 293: ©Dreamstime photos; pages 121, 124, 125, 127, 143, 181, 182, 188, 192, 208, 259: ©PhotoDisc; page 130: ©Suzuki; page 131: ©Bob Martin/Time Inc.; page 136: ©Graeme Teague; page 137: ©Lockheed Martin; pages 150, 206, 221-223, 249: ©Bruce Glassman; pages 152, 189, 195, 227, 228: ©photos.com; pages 155, 160, 180, 198, 202: ©Corel Corporation; pages 161, 169, 191, 194: ©Animals Animals; page 166: ©Norbert Wu; page 193: ©Photo Researchers, Inc.; page 230: ©Royal Gorge Bridge; page 233: ©Flickr; page 253: ©Robert Craig/The News Journal; page 255: ©Georgia Sports Hall of Fame; page 257: ©Stefano Carini; page 267: ©400 Monroe Associates; page 270: ©Uniform Photos; page 272: ©Jason and Clarence Lynch of EG Bear Company/Headline Books/ Martin and Delia Wach; page 274: ©Jim Carr; page 279: ©Scott Schauer; page 280: ©Twins Day Festivals; page 281: ©Elk Photography; page 283: ©Darlene Bordwell; page 287: ©Richard Bryant; page 292: ©George White; page 294: ©Noah's Ark.

Insert credits (clockwise from the top right corner of each section):
ENTERTAINMENT: (page 1) Photofest, Photofest, Photofest, AP; (page 2) AP, Photofest, AP, Photofest, AP, Photofest. SPORTS: (page 1) AP; (page 2) AP. ANIMALS: Dreamstime, Dreamstime, Animals Animals, Dreamstime, Animals Animals. ADVERTISING: Dreamstime, Dreamstime, John Grubb Photography, AP, Dreamstime.

THE
WORLD'S MOST
EMBARRASSING
RECORDS

ENTERTAINMENT
SPORTS ANIMALS
ADVERTISING

LUKE WILSON LOGAN LERMAN BRIE LARSON

It's time to stand up for the little guys.

BASED ON THE BESTSELLING NOVEL
HOOT

LOSING LOOT

In May 2006, *Hoot* opened in 3,018 theaters around the country and grossed only $3.36 million—an average of $1,116 per theater. This makes it the worst wide opening in history. The family comedy earned a total of $8.1 million, but cost about $15 million to make.

TRY AND TRY AGAIN

Was it really an honor just to be nominated—six times? Both Thelma Ritter and Deborah Kerr were each up for an Academy Award six times, but did not pick up a statue. Peter O'Toole has been nominated eight times and has yet to win the award. Luckily he decided to accept an honorary award for his lifetime work in 2003.

Thelma Ritter

A SINKING SHIP

In 2005, *Undiscovered* had a decent opening weekend, earning $676,048 in 754 theaters. However, one weekend later it earned just $91,748—an 86.4 percent drop! That's the biggest one-week drop in movie history.

Ashlee Simpson

SPOILED FRUIT

The Golden Raspberry Awards—or the Razzies—are the opposites of the Academy Awards, honoring the worst movies and actors of the year. The all-time Razzie champ is Sylvester Stallone with 30 nominations and 10 wins. The runner up is Madonna with 15 nominations and 9 wins.

PATIENCE PAYS OFF

After losing her first 18 nominations, soap star Susan Lucci finally won an award for number 19 in 1999. When her name was announced, she received a four-minute standing ovation. But her luck ended there. She's been nominated two more times, but lost both of those as well.

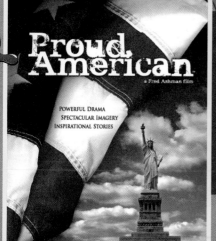

BOMBS AWAY

The worst per-theater average of a wide-release movie happened in 2008 with *Proud American*. The movie opened in 750 theaters and grossed $96,076—averaging just $128 per theater! And it didn't get much better after that. Its total gross was just $131,357.

MOVIE MONEY MELTDOWN

In 2001, the movie *Town & Country* opened and managed to gross $10.36 million worldwide. However, it cost $105 million. So *Town & Country* went down in movie history as the biggest money loser ever.

Godfather III

SEVEN IS NOT SO LUCKY

Both *The Godfather, Part III* (1991) and *Who's Afraid of Virginia Woolf?* (1967) were nominated for seven Golden Globe Awards. However, neither won a single statue. Although they have no awards to show for their hard work, they hold the honor of being the biggest losers in the history of the Golden Globes.

HELLO, IS ANYONE OUT THERE?

In 2008, the 80th Academy Awards became the most unwatched Oscars in history, averaging about 32 million viewers, or 18.6 percent of the audience share. This is mostly because none of the movies up for awards were hugely popular, and many of the stars honored were more popular in Europe.

ONE IS A LONELY NUMBER

Although it is an honor to be the number-one movie in America, *Jerry Maguire* wasn't celebrating too much. During the weekend of January 24–26, 1997, it took in just $5.5 million—the lowest amount for a number-one film in history.

NO PEEKING!

In 2007, the McLaren-Mercedes Formula 1 racing team was fined $100 million by the Fédération Internationale de L'Automobile for spying on the rival Ferrari team. This is one of the highest fines in sports history.

YOU'RE OUTTA HERE

Atlanta Braves coach Bobby Cox is one angry man. He has been thrown out of a record 143 baseball games. That's an average of about once every 29 games. At least he manages to do a good job when he gets to stay—he's listed as number four on the all-time managerial wins list.

SLIPPERY FINGERS

Quarterback Warren Moon is an amazing player, when he can hold on to the ball. While playing for the NFL from 1984 to 2000, Moon dropped the ball a record 161 times. His hands were especially slippery in 1990 and 1984, when he fumbled 18 and 17 times, respectively.

PLAY NICE

Watch out for Rasheed Wallace—he hits! The Detroit Pistons' Wallace set a single-season technical foul record in the 2000–01 season with 41 fouls. Oddly enough, he actually exceeded his own record from the previous season, when he made 38 technical fouls.

IT'S ALL IN THE NAME

Kentucky Derby horse Stone Street took his time while completing the race in 1908, finishing the 1.25 miles (2 km) in just over 2 minutes and 15 seconds. This is the slowest finish in history. Champion Secretariat ran the race in 1973 in just 1 minute and 59 seconds.

DUCK AND COVER

Pitcher Nolan Ryan must be the reason why batters are required to wear helmets. During his long and impressive career from 1966 to 1993, Ryan managed to throw 277 wild pitches. Not surprisingly, he has also walked 2,795 people—more than 50 percent more hitters than any other major league pitcher.

YOU HAVE TO ADMIRE THEIR DETERMINATION

The Detroit Lions had a tough time in 2008, ending the season with a record of 0–16. That's the worst record in NFL history. In fact, when the season ended, they had lost 23 of their last 24 games. Their biggest loss of the season came at the hands of the Tennessee Titans in November, with a score of 47–10.

SHARKS WITH NO BITE

During the 1992–93 season, the San Jose Sharks clinched the record for the most losses in one season with 71. And after a 17-game losing streak, the team also set a record that year for the most consecutive loses. It was just their second season as a major league hockey team, and they actually managed to make the play-offs just one year later.

FREE THROW AWAYS

Wilt Chamberlain missed 5,805 free throw attempts during his 1,045 games—the most misses in NBA history. This resulted in a free throw percentage of just .511. During a distinguished career that began in 1959, Chamberlain claimed many more impressive records, including being the only NBA player to score 100 points in a game (although probably not from free throws).

SCAREDY GOATS

When a fainting goat—a domestic breed found in the United States—is startled, its muscles freeze for about ten seconds. This painless condition affects young and old goats differently. Young goats just tip right over, while older goats learn to expect what's coming and can spread their legs for balance or lean against something.

TAKING ONE FOR THE TEAM

Malaysian ants are pretty crafty, although they don't live long enough to enjoy their success. These ants have glands full of poison in their bodies. When they feel threatened by nearby predators, they contract their abdomens and explode the glands, killing the predators and themselves in the process.

PROTECTED BY POOP

In order to keep from being eaten by predators, potato beetle larvae cover themselves with their own droppings. Not only is it stinky, but the beetles' droppings are actually poisonous when consumed.

ROOTIN' TOOTIN' BOVINES

About 90 percent of Australia's methane gas comes from the burping and flatulence of cows! A normal cow burps about 73.9 gallons (280 L) of gas each day. Considering that the country has about 27.5 million cows, that's approximately 2.0 billion gallons (7.5 billon L) of gas a day!

FREAKY FROGS

Hairy frogs have a secret weapon, even if they have to crack some bones to use them. When they are under attack, hairy frogs can break their own legs and push them through their toe pads, using them as supersharp claws. However, once the fight is over, it's hard to escape with two broken legs.

UNDESIRED UNDERWEAR

Bic created a marketing disaster when they decided to include underwear among their plastic products. Company officials thought that consumers might be as interested in disposable underwear as they were in the company's disposable pens, lighters, and razors. Unfortunately for Bic, this was not the case and the underwear was quickly discontinued.

PARCHED PETS DELIGHT

Pets entered a new era in pampering in 1994 when the Original Pet Drink Company in Florida started manufacturing bottled water for cats and dogs. Thirsty Cat was flavored like fish, while Thirsty Dog was flavored with beef. Both were actually approved for human consumption as well, and sold for $1.79 a bottle. However, most pet owners continued to fill up water bowls from the sink, and the company soon stopped production.

MIND OVER MATTER

Even though Life Savers candy continually ranks as a bestseller in the non-chocolate candy market, consumers weren't ready to fork over the cash for a Life Savers soda—in any of the five flavors. Even though it did fairly well in taste tests, the "liquid candy" soda was short-lived because consumers did not like the idea of drinking liquid candy.

THE WAVE THAT CRASHED

Despite Max Headroom's best efforts to get people to "catch the wave," when Coca-Cola introduced New Coke as a way to revive the company's popularity over Pepsi in 1985, it completely backfired. Consumers complained loudly, and the company quickly switched back to the original formula—now called Coca-Cola Classic—just three months later.

DITCHING THE DAIRY

Cosmopolitan is a very popular woman's magazine and a leader in the publishing industry. In 1999, they decided to build on this empire by launching a line of low-fat yogurt. Unfortunately, no one could figure out what magazines and dairy foods had in common, and the brand was pulled within 18 months.

Read for the World Record!

KIDS ANSWERED THE CHALLENGE!

Kids from every state and around the world participated in the *Scholastic Book Fairs Read for the World Record* challenge and set a record for summer reading!

Read for the World Record united students in an attempt to achieve a world record by reading for as many minutes as possible between May 1 and August 31, 2009.

CHECK OUT THESE COOL FACTS

STATES WITH THE HIGHEST VOLUME OF PARTICIPATION:

California	New York	Pennsylvania
Florida	Ohio	Texas

NUMBER OF SCHOOLS PARTICIPATING PER STATE

How many schools from your state participated?

STUDENTS FROM 35 COUNTRIES PARTICIPATED, INCLUDING:

Abu Dhabi	Egypt	Japan	Puerto Rico
Australia	Ethiopia	Mexico	Saudi Arabia
Canada	Ireland	Philippines	United Kingdom
China	Italy	Poland	Virgin Islands

CONGRATULATIONS TO EVERYONE WHO HELPED SET THE RECORD!

Total minutes read from May 1 to August 31, 2009

35,846,094

Total number of schools participating

8,725

Students from the top school, Sunset Palms Elementary, show off their minutes.

TOP **20** SCHOOLS WITH THE MOST READING MINUTES

Sunset Palms Elementary School of Boynton Beach, FL, was the school with the most reading minutes. Students there logged 683,057 minutes reading!

The following schools with organized Read for the World Record summer reading programs were also in the top 20:

Central Middle School	Columbus, IN
Charles E. Boger Elementary School	Kannapolis, NC
Glenwood Elementary School	Rutland, MA
Harmony School of Innovation	Houston, TX
Highland Elementary School	Lewiston, MO
Horizon Community Learning Center	Phoenix, AZ
Idea Frontier Academy	Brownsville, TX
Lake Norman Charter Middle School	Huntersville, NC
Mead Elementary School	Mead, CO
Midlakes Intermediate School	Clifton Springs, NY
Middle Canyon Elementary School	Tooele, UT
Oak Point Elementary School	Oak Point, TX
Onsted Elementary School	Onsted, MI
Ramsey Middle School	Louisville, KY
St. Isidore Elementary School	Danville, CA
Sun Valley Elementary School	Monroe, NC
Walt Disney Elementary School	Alvin, TX
Willamette Primary School	West Linn, OR
Wickersham Elementary School	Lancaster, PA